EXODUS EXPLAINED

EXODUS EXPLAINED
Understanding the Book and Its Message for Today

Samuel Whitaker

Part of the Bible for Modern Life Series

Ascent Press

Published by
Ascent Press

ISBN: 979-8-9997184-7-1

Printed in the United States of America

First Edition 2026

For those seeking clarity in the ancient words of Scripture.

CONTENTS

Disclaimer

This book provides an interpretive overview of the biblical text using historical scholarship and modern analysis tools. It is intended to help readers understand the themes, context, and message of the biblical narrative and is not intended to replace personal study of Scripture

Introduction

Why Exodus Still Matters

Exodus is one of the most dramatic and influential books in the entire Bible. It tells the story of a people trapped in oppression, a reluctant leader called by God, and a series of events that lead to liberation. At first glance, it reads like a historical account of Israel's escape from slavery in Egypt, but the book carries a deeper purpose. Exodus explores themes of liberation, identity, and the developing relationship between God and His people. It shows how a group of enslaved individuals becomes a nation with a shared purpose and a covenant with the God who rescues them. In doing so, Exodus becomes a foundational story not only for the people of Israel but also for understanding the larger message that runs throughout the entire Bible.

For many modern readers, however, Exodus can feel distant. The events described in the book took place thousands of years ago in a world that looks very different from our own. Ancient Egypt was a powerful empire built on rigid social structures, royal authority, and large-scale labor systems that depended on the work of slaves. The language of Pharaohs, plagues, burning bushes, and parted seas can feel far removed from everyday life in the modern world of technology, cities, and global communication. Because of this cultural and historical distance, some readers assume that Exodus belongs to a past era that has little connection to the present. Yet the foundational themes of the book remain remarkably relevant, addressing questions about suffering, justice, leadership, freedom, and the nature of God's involvement in human history.

At its core, Exodus asks a series of timeless questions that continue to shape how people think about life and faith. What does true freedom actually mean, and how is it different from simply escaping slavery? Why does suffering exist, and how does God respond when people cry out under injustice? What role do individuals play when they are called to lead or confront systems of power? And once deliverance comes, what does it mean to live as people who have been rescued and given a new identity? These questions are not limited to the ancient world. They remain deeply relevant to individuals and communities today, making Exodus one of the most enduring narratives in Scripture.

The book begins with Israel living under the harsh rule of Egypt, where generations of Hebrews have become enslaved within one of the most powerful civilizations of the ancient world. Pharaoh represents overwhelming authority, and the Israelites appear powerless within a system that treats them as expendable labor. Into this situation, God calls Moses, a reluctant and uncertain leader who becomes the central human figure in the story. Through Moses, God confronts Pharaoh and reveals His power through a dramatic sequence of events that includes the ten plagues, the institution of the Passover, and the eventual release of the Israelites from bondage. The narrative reaches a dramatic turning point when the people cross the Red Sea, leaving Egypt behind and beginning a journey toward a new future.

Yet the story does not end with the escape from Egypt. In many ways, the second half of Exodus focuses on what comes after deliverance. Freedom is not simply the absence of slavery; it requires learning how to live as a people shaped by God's presence and guidance. As the Israelites travel through the wilderness, they encounter challenges that test their faith, patience, and trust. During this journey, God establishes a covenant with them at Mount Sinai and gives them laws that will shape their identity as a nation. Among these instructions are the Ten

Commandments, which provide a framework for how the people are to relate both to God and to one another.

Because of these well-known moments, Exodus is often remembered as a collection of powerful individual stories: Moses standing before the burning bush, the devastating plagues falling upon Egypt, the night of the Passover, the waters of the Red Sea opening for the Israelites, and the dramatic giving of the law on Mount Sinai. Each of these events carries deep meaning and has been retold countless times in religious teaching, art, literature, and film. However, when these stories are viewed only as isolated episodes, it becomes easy to miss the larger narrative that connects them together.

Exodus is carefully structured to show a progression from oppression to freedom and from freedom to covenant. The early chapters reveal God as the one who hears the cries of the oppressed and acts to deliver them. The middle chapters display God's power over political authority and natural forces as Pharaoh is confronted and Egypt is shaken by the plagues. The later chapters shift the focus toward responsibility, showing that deliverance brings with it a new way of life centered on obedience, worship, and trust in God's presence. In this sense, the book moves from rescue to relationship, emphasizing that the goal of liberation is not simply escape, but transformation.

Understanding Exodus helps readers grasp the broader message of the Bible as a whole. The themes introduced here— deliverance from bondage, covenant between God and His people, and the ongoing presence of God among them—continue to appear throughout the rest of Scripture. The prophets frequently look back to the Exodus as the defining moment of God's saving power. The Psalms celebrate it as a reminder that God rescues His people. In the New Testament, the language of redemption and salvation echoes the story of liberation that begins in Egypt. Because of this, Exodus serves as a foundation for understanding how the Bible describes God's work in the world.

This book is designed to help modern readers approach Exodus with clarity and perspective. Instead of focusing primarily on academic debates, technical language, or complex theological arguments, the goal is to step back and see the big picture of what the book communicates. By exploring the historical background, the flow of the narrative, and the central themes that shape the story, readers can better understand why Exodus has remained such a significant text for thousands of years.

As we move through this exploration, we will consider the key questions that Exodus raises and the lessons that emerge from its narrative. What is the deeper meaning behind the dramatic events described in the book? How did these events shape the identity of the people of Israel? And what insights can modern readers gain from a story that took place in the distant past yet continues to influence faith, culture, and moral reflection today?

By the end of this journey, it becomes clear that Exodus is far more than an ancient account of a people escaping slavery. It is a story about how freedom begins with God's intervention, how identity forms through covenant and commitment, and how the path toward purpose often unfolds through struggle, uncertainty, and growth. The message of Exodus reminds readers that liberation is rarely simple and that the journey toward becoming who we are meant to be often begins in the most unlikely circumstances.

Chapter 1

The Human Question

"During that long period, the king of Egypt died. The Israelites groaned in their slavery and cried out, and their cry for help because of their slavery went up to God. God heard their groaning, and he remembered his covenant with Abraham, with Isaac, and with Jacob."
— Exodus 2:23–24

The Questions Behind the Bible's Story

Every major book of the Bible speaks to a real human question. These questions are not always stated directly, but they sit beneath the story and give it weight. Scripture does more than record events or preserve teachings. It speaks to the human condition— our fear, hope, failure, longing, and search for meaning in a world that often feels uncertain.

Genesis asks foundational questions about beginnings, identity, and the fractured relationship between God and humanity. It explains where the story starts and why the world is marked by both beauty and brokenness. By the end of Genesis, God has chosen a family through whom His purposes will continue, but that family is living in Egypt, and the future remains unresolved.

Exodus picks up that unfinished tension and asks a different question.

The Question at the Heart of Exodus

The central human question in Exodus is this: **What happens when people are trapped in circumstances they cannot escape on their own?**

That question reaches far beyond ancient Egypt. It touches something universal in human experience. People know what it is like to feel stuck, overpowered, or held in place by forces larger than themselves. Sometimes those forces are political or economic. Sometimes they are personal, relational, or spiritual. But the feeling is familiar: life narrows, options disappear, and freedom begins to feel far away.

Exodus begins there.

It begins with people who cannot simply fix what is wrong. They do not have the power to change the system over them. They cannot negotiate their way out. They cannot free themselves by strength alone. Their need is greater than improvement. Their need is deliverance.

Why People Feel Trapped

Human beings can become trapped in many ways. Entire societies can live under harsh rule, exploitation, or oppressive power. Communities can be boxed in by systems that reward the strong and burden the vulnerable. Individuals can also feel trapped by fear, grief, destructive habits, unhealthy relationships, debt, shame, or memories that continue to shape the present.

The details vary, but the experience is similar. People may feel that forces are controlling their lives that they cannot overcome. They may still function, work, and survive, but inwardly they know they are not free.

That is part of what makes Exodus so enduring. It does not begin with people asking for a better version of the life they already have. It begins with people who know something is deeply wrong and who cannot solve it on their own.

The Longing for Rescue

When people live under pressure long enough, one of two things often happens. Some give up and assume nothing will ever change. Others hold on to the hope that somehow, someday, life could be different.

Exodus speaks to that second instinct. It gives voice to the longing for rescue.

That longing appears across human history. People long to be released from what diminishes them. They want relief from fear, injustice, bondage, and systems that strip away dignity. They want to believe that the future does not have to look exactly like the past.

That desire is not weakness. It is part of being human. People were not made to live crushed by fear, dehumanized by power, or defined forever by what enslaves them. Exodus begins with that cry.

Why Freedom Is Not a Simple Idea

Yet Exodus also pushes the question further. It does not ask only how people get out of bondage. It also asks what freedom is for.

That matters because many people assume freedom means the removal of pressure, pain, or limits. In one sense, it does. But Exodus shows that freedom is not only escape. Freedom creates new questions.

What happens after the old chains are broken?
How should people live once they are no longer under the old master?
What kind of identity replaces survival?
What will guide people when fear no longer sets the agenda?

These are harder questions than they first appear. Many people want change, but fewer are prepared for the responsibility that change requires.

The Fear of the Unknown

There is another tension at the heart of Exodus: sometimes people long for freedom and fear it at the same time.

This is part of real life. Even painful situations can become familiar. People may hate what is crushing them and still hesitate to leave it, because the unknown feels dangerous. A familiar misery can seem safer than an unfamiliar future.

That is one reason transformation is rarely easy. Freedom is not just about leaving something behind. It is also about stepping into a life that has not yet fully taken shape. That kind of movement requires trust, courage, and endurance.

Exodus understands that tension. It does not present human beings as simple creatures who always welcome change once it appears. It shows that people can pray for deliverance and still struggle when deliverance begins to come.

A Pattern That Repeats in Human Life

This pattern shows up again and again. People cry out for change, but when change starts disrupting what is familiar, fear rises. They may question whether the old life was really so bad. They may doubt the path ahead. They may wonder if freedom is worth the cost.

That is not unusual. It is human.

Exodus is important because it tells the truth about that process. The journey from bondage to freedom is not clean or instant. It is often marked by uncertainty, setbacks, resistance, and the slow work of learning to live differently.

That makes the book deeply relevant. Exodus is not only about ancient injustice. It is about the painful, necessary movement from captivity to trust, from fear to obedience, and from survival to identity.

The Deeper Human Question

The deeper human question in Exodus is not merely, **How do we get free?**

It is this: **How does freedom begin, and what does it require of us once it comes?**

That question drives the book forward. Exodus will show people crying out, being delivered, struggling in the wilderness, and learning what it means to live under God's guidance rather than Pharaoh's control. But before the story unfolds, the question must be felt.

What do people do when they are trapped?
Where do they turn when their strength is not enough?
What happens when rescue comes, but the road ahead is still hard?
How does a people shaped by oppression learn to live in freedom?
Those are the questions Exodus forces into the open.

Why Exodus Still Matters

That is why Exodus still speaks with force today. It speaks to anyone who has felt pinned down by circumstances, power, fear, grief, sin, or suffering. It speaks to those who have cried out for change. It speaks to those who have discovered that getting out is only the beginning.

Exodus reminds readers that freedom is real, but it is not shallow. It is a gift, a disruption, and a calling. It breaks old chains, but it also begins the harder work of becoming a different kind of person.

That is the human question behind the book. Not simply whether liberation is possible, but what it means to be led out of bondage and into a new way of life.

Chapter 2

Orientation

"But the more they were oppressed, the more they multiplied and spread; so the Egyptians came to dread the Israelites."
— Exodus 1:12

The Story Continues After Genesis

Exodus is the second book of the Bible and continues the story that began in Genesis. Rather than introducing a completely new narrative, Exodus builds directly upon the events and relationships that developed in the earlier story of Israel's beginnings. The book assumes that readers already understand the background established in Genesis, and it moves forward from that foundation to describe how the descendants of the patriarchs become a nation with a distinct identity and purpose.

This continuity matters because Exodus is not simply the next book in sequence. It is the next movement in a larger story. The people who suffer in Egypt are not strangers to the reader. They are the descendants of Abraham, Isaac, and Jacob. They carry with them the memory of promises that stretch back generations. God had pledged to bless Abraham, multiply his descendants, and give them a land of their own. Those promises form the background of Exodus, even when the people themselves appear far removed from their fulfillment.

Genesis concludes with the account of Joseph, one of the sons of Jacob, who rose to a position of influence within Egypt after interpreting Pharaoh's dreams and helping the nation prepare for a devastating famine. Through wisdom and careful planning, Joseph organized a system that allowed Egypt to store grain during years of abundance so that the nation could survive the years of scarcity that followed. Because of Joseph's role in preserving Egypt during that crisis, Pharaoh honored him and welcomed his family into the land.

Joseph's father, Jacob, and his brothers settled in Egypt during that period of famine. What began as a temporary refuge soon became a long-term home for their descendants. The family was given land where they could live and raise their flocks, and for a time, their presence in Egypt was viewed positively because of Joseph's service to the nation. This moment represents one of the final scenes in Genesis, where the descendants of Abraham find themselves living in a foreign land but still carrying the promises God made to their ancestors.

There is already tension in that ending. The family of promise is alive, protected, and growing, yet they are not in the land that had been promised to them. They are in Egypt, dependent upon circumstances that may not remain stable forever. That tension becomes the starting point for Exodus. What seemed like provision in one generation becomes burden in the next. What served as refuge eventually becomes the setting of bondage.

Exodus opens several generations after those events. By this time, the Israelites, once a small extended family living peacefully in Egypt, had multiplied into a large and growing population. The book begins by reminding readers of this expansion, emphasizing that the descendants of Jacob have become numerous and increasingly visible within Egyptian society. Their presence is no longer limited to a small group connected to Joseph's household. Instead, they have grown into a distinct people whose numbers are large enough to attract attention.

This growth is important for more than historical reasons. It also signals that God's promise to multiply Abraham's descendants has continued even in a foreign land. The people are increasing, but their growth does not immediately lead to blessings or stability. Instead, it contributes to fear within Egypt. This pattern appears often in Scripture. God's purposes continue moving forward, but not always in ways that seem secure or obvious at the time. In Exodus, growth becomes the very thing that provokes hostility. The promise continues, but the path becomes harder.

The opening of the book establishes the basic orientation readers need. Exodus is a story about the descendants of promise living in a place of oppression. It is about what happens when God's people are caught in circumstances that seem to contradict the future spoken over them. It is also about how God acts when human systems appear stronger than human hope.

A Changing Political Landscape

Over the years that followed Joseph's death, the political landscape of Egypt changed significantly. The generation that remembered Joseph and the benefits he brought to the nation gradually passed away. Historical memory fades, and the connection between Joseph's actions and the Israelites living in Egypt becomes less significant to those who come later. Eventually, a new Pharaoh rises to power who does not share the sense of gratitude that once existed toward Joseph and his family.

This change in leadership is one of the most important turning points in the opening chapters of Exodus. It reminds readers that human governments are unstable and that the favor enjoyed in one generation may disappear in the next. Political memory is often short. Acts of service that once brought honor can quickly lose their influence when new rulers emerge with different concerns and priorities.

This new ruler does not view the Israelites through the same lens as the previous generation. Instead of seeing them as helpful residents within the empire, he begins to see them as a potential threat. Their population has grown large enough that Pharaoh becomes concerned about what might happen if they were to align themselves with Egypt's enemies during a time of conflict. From his perspective, their numbers and cultural differences create the possibility that they might undermine the security of the kingdom.

In the ancient world, political leaders often worried about large minority populations living within their borders. If a conflict arose with neighboring nations, these groups could potentially side with an outside power and destabilize the kingdom from within. Pharaoh's fear reflects this kind of thinking. He interprets the Israelites' growing population not as a sign of prosperity but as a risk that must be managed before it becomes dangerous.

Fear often distorts moral judgment. Instead of responding to the Israelites as people, Pharaoh begins to respond to them as a problem. Once that shift takes place, tyranny becomes easier to justify. The opening chapters of Exodus show how political fear can turn neighbors into threats and populations into tools of state control. The issue is no longer gratitude for Joseph's past service. The issue becomes the preservation of Egyptian power.

This political shift also changes the emotional atmosphere of the story. The Israelites are no longer living in a season shaped by remembered favor. They are living in a season shaped by suspicion. The same empire that once protected them now sees them as expendable. This is how Exodus begins to move from family story to national crisis.

From Hospitality to Oppression

In response to these fears, Pharaoh implements policies designed to control and weaken the Israelites. Rather than expelling them from Egypt, he chooses a strategy that will keep them under close supervision while also benefiting the empire. The Israelites are subjected to forced labor, with the expectation that harsh working conditions will limit their strength and slow their population growth.

Under this system, the Israelites are placed under the authority of Egyptian taskmasters who monitor their work and enforce strict discipline. They are required to build storage cities and infrastructure projects that support the expansion and wealth of the Egyptian empire. Their labor contributes to the construction of buildings, supply centers, and other facilities that strengthen the economic and political stability of the nation.

Over time, their daily lives become defined by physical labor, strict oversight, and the loss of personal freedom. What began as a relationship of hospitality and cooperation gradually turned into a system of exploitation and forced labor. The people who once lived peacefully in Egypt now find themselves trapped within a structure designed to control their lives and extract their labor.

The movement from hospitality to domination is one of the clearest examples in Exodus of how power can reshape relationships. A people welcomed for one reason can later be used for another. This also shows that injustice does not always begin all at once. It often begins with policies justified as necessary, practical, or protective. Over time, those policies harden into a system that dehumanizes the people it controls.

For the Israelites, this change would have been deeply disorienting. Their identity within Egypt had shifted dramatically. They were no longer guests living under protection. They were now workers living under coercion. The social and political environment around them had changed, and with it their daily experience of life.

Yet even here, the narrative is doing more than describing suffering. It is also preparing the reader to understand why liberation will matter so much. The harsher the system becomes, the clearer it is that the people cannot simply improve their situation through ordinary means. Their condition is not a temporary inconvenience. It is a bondage.

Escalating Fear and Harsh Policies

Despite these attempts to control the population, the Israelites continue to grow in number. Their increasing population only intensifies Pharaoh's concerns. Instead of weakening them, the harsh labor appears to coincide with continued growth. From Pharaoh's perspective, this development reinforces the fear that the Israelites may eventually become too numerous to control.

As a result, Pharaoh introduces even harsher measures. The policies that were originally intended to manage the Israelites gradually evolved into strategies designed to suppress them more aggressively. Pharaoh eventually commands that Hebrew male infants be killed at birth, hoping that this brutal policy will reduce the future strength of the Israelite population.

This moment reveals the depth of Pharaoh's fear and the extreme lengths he is willing to pursue in order to maintain control over the situation. The decree transforms the oppression of the Israelites from forced labor into something even more severe. The future of the people is now directly threatened, and every Hebrew family lives under the shadow of this dangerous command.

There is a clear moral descent here. What begins as political anxiety becomes state-sponsored cruelty. Pharaoh is no longer merely trying to manage a workforce. He is now attempting to control the future of an entire people through violence. The narrative exposes how unchecked fear, joined to power, can produce inhuman policies.

This escalation also sets the stage for the introduction of Moses. The darker the environment becomes, the more significant his survival appears. Exodus often moves this way. Pressure increases before deliverance appears. The crisis deepens before the turning point emerges. The birth of Moses comes not in a neutral setting but at the height of danger.

The Birth of Moses

Against this dark and dangerous backdrop, the story introduces one of its most important figures: Moses. His birth takes place during the period when Pharaoh's decree threatens the lives of Hebrew boys, placing him immediately in danger from the moment he enters the world. The circumstances surrounding his birth highlight both the severity of the situation and the courage of those who resist the decree.

Through a series of courageous decisions made by his mother and others who protect him, Moses survives the threat that hangs over Hebrew children. His mother hides him as long as possible and eventually places him in a basket along the Nile River, hoping that someone will find him and spare his life. In an unexpected turn of events, the child is discovered by Pharaoh's daughter.

Instead of following the decree that threatens Hebrew infants, Pharaoh's daughter chooses to adopt the child. Moses is brought into the royal household and raised within the environment of Egyptian power and authority. The child who was meant to be destroyed by Pharaoh's command now grows up within the very palace that represents Egyptian rule.

This is one of the great ironies of the book. The system that seeks to destroy Hebrew sons becomes the setting in which the future deliverer is preserved and prepared. Moses survives not because the danger is small, but because courage, compassion, and providence converge in a way no one could have predicted.

His survival also introduces a recurring biblical pattern: God's work often begins quietly, in hidden and vulnerable ways, before it becomes visible on a larger scale. The man who will one day confront Pharaoh enters the story as an endangered child, dependent on the courage of others.

Moses Between Two Worlds

Moses grows up with a unique perspective shaped by both his Hebrew heritage and his upbringing within the Egyptian court. On one hand, he receives the education and privileges associated with life in the royal household. On the other hand, he remains connected to his identity as a Hebrew and becomes aware of the suffering endured by his people.

As Moses becomes an adult, this tension becomes increasingly difficult to ignore. One day, he witnesses an Egyptian official mistreating a Hebrew laborer. The injustice of the moment provokes a strong response, and Moses intervenes in the conflict. In the course of that confrontation, he kills the Egyptian, an action that quickly becomes known.

Realizing that his actions will bring punishment from Pharaoh, Moses flees Egypt. His departure marks the beginning of a long period of exile. He travels to the region of Midian, where he begins a new life far removed from the political center of Egypt and from the people he once knew.

Moses' position between two worlds is important because it shapes the kind of leader he will become. He understands the power of Egypt from the inside, yet he also knows the suffering of the Hebrews. He belongs fully to neither world, which makes his life unsettled but also uniquely fitted for the role he will later assume.

His flight to Midian also shows that calling does not always emerge immediately from early passion or moral impulse. Moses reacts against tyranny, but his first attempt does not lead to deliverance. Instead, it leads to exile. The path toward his true calling will require time, humility, and transformation.

The Encounter at the Burning Bush

Years pass as Moses lives in this new environment. He marries, starts a family, and works as a shepherd tending flocks in the wilderness. The man who once lived in Pharaoh's household now spends his days in quiet isolation far from the power structures of Egypt.

It is during this period of exile that Moses experiences one of the most dramatic and significant moments in the entire narrative of Exodus. While tending sheep in the wilderness, he encounters a bush that appears to be burning yet is not consumed by the flames. As he approaches to investigate, God speaks to him from within the fire.

Through this extraordinary event, God reveals His intention to deliver the Israelites from their suffering in Egypt. Moses is called to return to the very place he fled and to confront Pharaoh with the demand that the Israelites be allowed to leave their bondage. The quiet life Moses has built in the wilderness is suddenly interrupted by a mission that will change the course of his life and the future of his people.

This moment reorients the whole story. Up to this point, readers have watched the suffering of Israel and the shaping of Moses. At the burning bush, those two lines converge. The hidden work of preparation meets the public work of calling. Moses is no longer merely a survivor or exile. He is now a messenger, sent back into the center of the crisis he once escaped.

Moses the Reluctant Leader

From that point forward, Moses becomes the central human figure in the story. At first, he expresses hesitation and doubt about his ability to fulfill this role. He questions whether he possesses the authority or the skills necessary to confront Pharaoh and lead a nation of people out of slavery.

Despite these doubts, Moses ultimately accepts the responsibility placed before him. Through Moses, God challenges Pharaoh's authority and demonstrates His power through a series of dramatic events that will ultimately lead to Israel's freedom. Moses becomes the mediator between God and the people, communicating God's instructions, guiding the Israelites through their journey, and helping establish the foundation for their life as a nation.

This reminds readers that biblical leadership is not usually built on personal confidence alone. Moses does not volunteer because he sees himself as the obvious choice. He becomes a leader because he is called, challenged, corrected, and sustained by God. That pattern adds depth to the book's understanding of leadership. Strength matters, but dependence matters more.

The Journey Toward a New Identity

As the narrative unfolds, Moses leads the Israelites out of slavery and into a new phase of their history. Their departure from Egypt becomes one of the defining events in the identity of the people of Israel. Future generations will look back on this moment as the time when God delivered them from bondage and established them as His people.

However, the journey does not end with their escape from Egypt. Instead, their deliverance marks the beginning of a longer process in which they must learn how to live as a community guided by God's presence and instruction. Freedom opens the door to a new future, but it also requires the development of new patterns of life and responsibility.

This is one of the key orientation points for the whole book: Exodus is not only about getting out of Egypt. It is about becoming a people. The escape is only the beginning; the formation that follows is just as essential.

The Structure of the Book

The structure of the book of Exodus reflects this progression in the story. Although the narrative contains many individual episodes and important moments, the overall movement of the book can be understood in three major sections that follow the development of Israel's journey from bondage to covenant.

Oppression and Calling

The first section focuses on Israel's oppression in Egypt and the calling of Moses. These chapters describe the harsh conditions under which the Israelites live, the policies implemented by Pharaoh to control them, and the circumstances surrounding Moses' birth and early life. They also introduce the moment when Moses encounters God at the burning bush and receives the mission to return to Egypt and lead the people out of slavery.

Confrontation and Deliverance

The second section centers on the dramatic confrontation between Moses and Pharaoh and the events that lead to the Exodus from Egypt. During this portion of the narrative, Moses repeatedly delivers God's message to Pharaoh, demanding that the Israelites be allowed to leave. Pharaoh's refusal leads to a series of powerful signs and plagues that challenge his authority and reveal God's power over the forces that Egypt once trusted for stability and prosperity. These events ultimately culminate in the Passover and the departure of the Israelites from Egypt.

Covenant and Identity

The third major section of the book shifts the focus toward the journey of the Israelites through the wilderness and their arrival at Mount Sinai. During this phase of the narrative, the people begin to learn what it means to live as a nation under God's guidance. At Mount Sinai, they received the covenant, including the Ten Commandments and additional instructions that would shape their identity and their relationship with God.

Each of these sections builds on the previous one and contributes to the overall message of the book. The story begins with forced labor and the desperate circumstances of a people trapped within a powerful empire. It then moves into the dramatic events that lead to liberation and the departure from Egypt. Finally, the narrative turns toward the formation of identity, as the Israelites begin to understand what it means to live as a people bound together by a covenant with God.

Seen this way, Exodus is not simply a rescue story. It is a carefully shaped narrative of movement—from bondage to freedom, from fear to trust, from scattered descendants to covenant community. That larger orientation helps readers see why the book matters so much within the Bible. It is not only a story about what God did once. It is a story about how God forms a people for Himself.

Chapter 3

The World Behind the Book

"God said to Moses, 'I am who I am.' This is what you are to
say to the Israelites: 'I AM has sent me to you.'"
— Exodus 3:14

Understanding the Historical Setting

To understand Exodus more fully, it is helpful to consider the historical and cultural world in which the story unfolds. The events described in the book did not occur in isolation but within the context of one of the most sophisticated and influential civilizations of the ancient world. The customs, beliefs, and political structures of that society shaped the environment in which the Israelites lived and the circumstances they faced. When modern readers imagine the events of Exodus, they often picture individual scenes—Pharaoh's palace, the plagues, the Red Sea— but these events were deeply connected to the broader world in which they occurred.

Examining the historical background helps readers appreciate the magnitude of the story. The narrative of Exodus describes a conflict between a group of enslaved people and the most powerful ruler of their region. Understanding the world of ancient Egypt allows readers to see why the events of the book would have appeared astonishing to those who first experienced them. What might appear today as a familiar religious story would have represented a dramatic challenge to one of the strongest and most stable civilizations of the ancient world.

Historical setting also helps readers avoid flattening the book into a simple moral tale. Exodus is not merely about one bad ruler and one oppressed group. It is about a people living under the weight of a massive political and religious system that shaped nearly every part of life. Egypt was not just a place on a map. It was an organized empire with long-standing traditions, visible wealth, military power, and a worldview that gave spiritual meaning to its political order. The more clearly readers understand that, the more powerfully the book itself comes into focus.

This kind of background does not replace the message of Exodus. It sharpens it. It helps readers see why the deliverance of Israel would have seemed so unlikely and why the events described in the narrative would have carried such significance for those who first told and retold the story. The God who acts in Exodus is not confronting a weak local ruler or a minor social problem. He is confronting one of the most impressive human systems the ancient world had produced.

Egypt as a World Power

Egypt in the ancient world was one of the most powerful and stable civilizations of its time. For centuries, it maintained a strong centralized government, advanced agricultural systems supported by the annual flooding of the Nile River, and impressive architectural achievements that still capture attention today. The Nile played a central role in the life of the nation, providing water for agriculture and transportation while creating fertile soil that supported large populations.

Because of the Nile's predictable flooding cycle, Egyptian farmers were able to grow crops consistently, which allowed the nation to develop a strong and reliable food supply. This agricultural stability helped Egypt become a prosperous and influential kingdom. Surpluses of grain and other resources allowed the government to support large cities, organize major construction projects, and maintain military strength.

Massive temples, monuments, and pyramids demonstrated the wealth and organizational strength of the empire. These structures were not only architectural achievements but also symbols of national identity and political power. The ability to mobilize large numbers of workers and resources for construction projects showed the effectiveness of Egypt's administrative system and the authority of its rulers.

Egyptian society also possessed a highly developed system of administration that allowed the government to manage resources, organize large construction projects, and maintain order across a wide territory. Officials recorded agricultural production, monitored labor forces, and coordinated trade and taxation. Because of these factors, Egypt was often viewed by neighboring peoples as a symbol of strength, stability, and prosperity.

This is important for reading Exodus because it means Israel's tyranny took place inside a system that appeared immovable. Egypt was not fragile. It was not improvising from one crisis to the next. It was orderly, established, and accustomed to controlling its environment. To the outside world, Egypt likely looked like the kind of civilization that would endure indefinitely. Its fields produced food, its river sustained life, its monuments projected permanence, and its rulers exercised visible authority over land and labor alike.

The Exodus story does not begin in a setting where change seems likely. It begins in a setting where change seems impossible. The people of Israel are not trapped in a weak society about to collapse. They are trapped in a society that appears too strong to be challenged. This is one reason the book emphasizes God's intervention so clearly. Humanly speaking, the balance of power is overwhelmingly one-sided.

Egypt's position as a world power also shaped how it viewed itself. Prosperity often reinforces confidence, and confidence can turn into pride. The empire's wealth, military capacity, and cultural sophistication likely supported the belief that Egypt's order was not only strong but right. From within such a worldview, a demand to release a major labor force would not have sounded merely inconvenient. It would have sounded absurd, dangerous, and contrary to the logic of empire itself.

The Role of Pharaoh

At the center of this powerful society stood Pharaoh, the ruler of Egypt. Pharaoh was not viewed merely as a political leader in the way modern societies understand kings or presidents. Instead, he was regarded as a divine figure who represented the gods and maintained the order of the universe. Egyptians believed that Pharaoh's authority was closely connected to the stability of the world itself.

In Egyptian thought, maintaining harmony within the universe was essential. The concept, often referred to as *ma'at,* represented balance, order, and justice in the world. Pharaoh was believed to uphold this balance through both political leadership and religious responsibility. His role included not only governing the nation but also ensuring that harmony existed between the gods, the land, and the people.

Because of this belief, Pharaoh's power extended beyond politics into religion and culture, making his authority appear absolute within Egyptian society. To challenge Pharaoh was not simply to oppose a political ruler; it was to challenge a figure believed to have divine authority. This understanding helps explain why Pharaoh's refusal to release the Israelites becomes such a significant conflict within the narrative of Exodus.

The conflict between Moses and Pharaoh carries greater weight than a simple political disagreement. Moses does not merely arrive with an alternative policy proposal. He comes with a word from a different authority altogether. That is why the repeated demand to let the people go is so threatening. It places

Pharaoh in the position of either submitting to a higher authority or hardening himself against it.

From Pharaoh's perspective, yielding would not only mean losing labor. It would mean admitting that his own claims to sacred authority had limits. Within a culture that tied royal power to cosmic stability, that would have been a deeply humiliating possibility. Pharaoh's resistance in Exodus is therefore not just stubbornness in a personal sense. It is the resistance of a system defending its entire understanding of power and legitimacy.

This also helps readers understand why the narrative repeatedly emphasizes God's signs, wonders, and judgments. The issue is not simply whether Pharaoh will make a practical decision. The issue is whether Egypt's ruler will recognize that he is not the ultimate. Each act of divine intervention exposes the limits of Pharaoh's authority. Each refusal intensifies the conflict. The story unfolds not only as a struggle over labor and freedom, but as a confrontation over who truly rules.

Religion and Daily Life

This understanding of Pharaoh shaped the structure of the entire civilization. Religion, politics, and daily life were deeply intertwined, and the boundaries between them were often difficult to separate. Egyptian culture viewed the world as a place filled with divine activity, where the gods influenced natural forces, human events, and the success of the nation.

Temples served as centers of both worship and economic activity. Priests held critical positions within the society, overseeing rituals and maintaining the temples that honored the gods. These temples also managed land, resources, and labor, making them influential institutions within the broader economy.

Religious rituals were believed to influence everything from agricultural success to national security. Offerings, ceremonies, and festivals were performed regularly to maintain the favor of the gods and ensure the continued prosperity of the land. Within this worldview, maintaining the proper relationship between humans and the divine world was essential for the stability of society.

The Egyptians maintained a complex system of gods associated with natural forces such as the sun, the Nile River, animals, weather patterns, and the cycles of life and death. Each deity represented different aspects of nature and human experience. Together they formed a religious system that explained the functioning of the world and the responsibilities of its inhabitants.

Within this worldview, the gods were believed to maintain balance in the universe, and Pharaoh served as their representative on earth.

This religious framework meant that daily life in Egypt was never simply ordinary. Agriculture, government, ritual, birth, death, and kingship all carried sacred meaning. The natural world was not seen as neutral or accidental. It was filled with divine associations. The river that watered the land, the sun that marked time and light, the animals used in labor or worship, and the cycles of fertility and death were all understood within a spiritual framework.

That's important for reading Exodus because the plagues do not strike a secular society. They strike a culture that interprets nature, prosperity, and kingship through religion. When the Nile becomes a source of crisis rather than life, or darkness interrupts the normal order of the land, the disruption is not merely practical. It is theological. It calls into question the reliability of the gods, the stability of the world they were believed to govern, and the authority of the ruler who claimed to mediate that order.

For the Israelites living inside this world, the difference between Egyptian religion and the God who speaks to Moses would have mattered profoundly. They were not simply living in a foreign country. They were living inside a foreign worldview. Exodus shows what happens when the God of Israel reveals

Himself as not one divine force among many, but as Lord over all the things Egypt thought it understood.

Labor, Construction, and Power

Within such a system, maintaining order and productivity was essential to the strength of the empire. Large building projects were a defining feature of Egyptian culture, and these projects required significant labor forces. Temples, cities, irrigation systems, and storage facilities were constructed on a massive scale, demonstrating both the resources available to Egypt and the organizational ability of its leaders.

These projects served multiple purposes. They reinforced the authority of Pharaoh, honored the gods through monumental architecture, and supported the economic needs of the empire. Large storage cities, for example, allowed Egypt to store grain and supplies that could be used during times of scarcity or distributed to workers and soldiers.

The construction of such projects required large groups of laborers working under strict supervision. This demand for labor created systems in which certain populations were assigned the responsibility of performing physically demanding work that supported the broader goals of the empire.

In a society like Egypt, construction was never merely functional. Monumental building was a visible expression of order, control, and greatness. Every city, storage center, and temple communicated something about who held power and how stable that power appeared. The labor behind those structures was therefore politically significant. To control labor was to strengthen the empire's image and expand its capacity.

This is why the harsh rule of Israel cannot be separated from Egypt's larger ambitions. The people are not being worked at random. Their labor is feeding the machinery of empire. They are helping build the very system that keeps them in bondage. That makes their situation even more bitter. Their strength is being used to reinforce the authority that limits their freedom.

When Exodus describes the labor of Israel, it is also telling readers something about the nature of oppressive systems. Such systems often depend on the very people they diminish. They draw strength from those they control and use human effort to reinforce structures of inequality. That is why liberation in Exodus must include more than emotional encouragement. It must involve actual release from the machinery of forced labor itself.

Slavery in the Ancient World

Slavery and forced labor were common features of many ancient societies, including Egypt. Empires often relied on large populations of laborers to complete construction projects, cultivate fields, and support the economy. In many cases, conquered peoples or minority populations were assigned these roles, particularly when rulers believed that such groups might otherwise become a political threat.

By placing these populations under strict supervision and assigning them heavy labor, leaders could both control their movements and benefit from their work. Taskmasters monitored productivity and enforced discipline, ensuring that projects were completed according to the demands of the state.

While conditions could vary depending on the time and location, the system of forced labor often involved difficult working environments and limited freedom for those subjected to it. The purpose of such systems was not only economic but also political, as they helped maintain control over large and diverse populations within the empire.

This broader ancient context helps modern readers understand that the oppression in Exodus was not unusual by the standards of the empire. What was unusual was not that a great power used forced labor. What was unusual was that the God of a subjected people intervened so decisively against that system. Empires enslaving vulnerable populations were tragically common. An empire being publicly humbled on behalf of those people was not.

That distinction matters because it highlights the theological force of the book. Exodus does not pretend the world was fair. It shows readers a world in which coercion, fear, and exploitation were normal features of political life. Yet into that world, God acts. He hears, sees, remembers, and delivers. The historical harshness of the setting makes the message of the book more, not less, powerful.

Israel's Place in Egypt

The Israelites appear to have become one such labor group within Egypt. Over time, they transitioned from welcomed residents into a population subjected to forced labor and strict oversight. Egyptian authorities organized their work through systems of taskmasters who monitored productivity and enforced harsh working conditions.

The Israelites were required to build cities and infrastructure that strengthened the Egyptian empire while receiving little freedom in return. Their labor supported projects that symbolized Egyptian power and prosperity, even as their own lives became increasingly restricted.

Their situation illustrates how powerful societies in the ancient world could use minority populations as sources of labor while maintaining control through political and social pressure. What began as a peaceful relationship between Joseph's family and the Egyptian government gradually transformed into a system of enslavement that shaped the lives of future generations.

Their position in Egypt was therefore both socially vulnerable and politically useful. They were numerous enough to be feared, yet not powerful enough to defend themselves. They could be exploited precisely because they existed within the reach of the empire but outside the centers of power that defined it.

This helps explain why the story of Exodus is so deeply concerned with identity. The Israelites are not merely overworked. They are a people in danger of being defined entirely by what Egypt requires from them. Forced labor reduces their ability to function. Deliverance will have to restore more than movement. It will have to restore identity, memory, and purpose.

Why the Exodus Was So Shocking

Understanding this historical background helps readers appreciate the dramatic tension within the story of Exodus. The Israelites were not simply living under a harsh local ruler but under the authority of one of the most powerful empires of their time. The structures of Egyptian society reinforced Pharaoh's authority, and the belief that he represented the gods made resistance seem nearly impossible.

Within this context, the idea that a group of enslaved laborers could challenge Pharaoh and leave the empire would have appeared extraordinary. Egypt's strength, organization, and religious authority made it seem invincible. The possibility that this empire could be disrupted by the actions described in Exodus would have seemed almost unimaginable.

For the Israelites themselves, the shock would likely have been even greater. Generations had lived under Egyptian control. The routines of slavery had become normal. When people live under a system for long enough, even their imagination can become limited by it. They may hope for relief, but they may not truly expect the whole structure to be overturned.

That is why Exodus unfolds with so much emphasis on signs, conflict, repetition, and escalation. The story does not describe a minor shift in political policy. It describes the unraveling of an entire way of understanding power. The more impressive Egypt appears at the beginning, the more astonishing the deliverance becomes by the time it unfolds.

The Meaning of the Plagues

The plagues described in Exodus also take on deeper meaning when viewed within the cultural and religious framework of ancient Egypt. Each plague affects an aspect of the natural world that held symbolic or religious significance within Egyptian belief systems.

Elements such as the Nile River, animals, weather patterns, and the environment were closely connected to specific gods within Egyptian religion. These associations meant that natural events were often interpreted as reflections of divine power or favor.

Many scholars have noted that the plagues appear to challenge these elements directly. The Nile, which was central to Egyptian agriculture and life, becomes a source of disruption. Animals that were associated with certain deities appear within the plagues in ways that undermine their symbolic power. Even the sun, an important element within Egyptian religious belief, is affected during the plague of darkness.

When these events are considered within their historical context, they reveal an additional dimension to the narrative.

The plagues are not random displays of force. They are targeted disruptions of the very order Egypt trusted. The water, land, animals, weather, health, light, and firstborn all belong to spheres that seemed woven into the stability of Egyptian life. As those things are struck one after another, the message becomes clearer: the God of Israel is not limited, threatened, or outranked by the powers Egypt reveres.

This is one reason the conflict intensifies the way it does. Pharaoh is not only being asked to release a labor force. He is being shown that his world is not as secure as he believes. Every plague exposes a weakness in the system. Every refusal hardens the confrontation. By the end, Egypt is not merely inconvenienced. Its confidence is shattered.

A Challenge to Egyptian Beliefs

The plagues demonstrate that the God of Israel is not limited by the systems of belief that shaped Egyptian society. Rather than operating within the framework of Egyptian religion, the narrative portrays God as possessing authority over the natural world and over the structures of the empire itself.

Each event reinforces the idea that the power Pharaoh claimed to represent is ultimately subordinate to a greater authority. For those witnessing the events described in the story, this would have represented a dramatic challenge to the worldview that defined Egyptian culture.

The conflict between Moses and Pharaoh becomes more than a political struggle. It becomes a confrontation between competing understandings of power, authority, and the nature of the divine.

Egypt assumed that the world was held together by a network of powers that Pharaoh helped preserve. Exodus declares that the world is ruled by the God who speaks, judges, remembers, and saves. That difference is enormous. It means Israel's deliverance is not simply a national victory. It is a theological revelation. It reveals who God is by showing what Egypt is not.

Seeing the Story Clearly

Understanding the ancient world in which Exodus takes place allows modern readers to see the narrative with greater clarity. The events described in the book were not merely dramatic moments within a story but actions that disrupted a powerful political and religious system.

For the Israelites, these events would have demonstrated that their God was capable of confronting the most powerful empire they knew and bringing about their deliverance.

When readers recognize the strength of Egypt's civilization, the authority attributed to Pharaoh, and the deep connection between religion and political power within that culture, the story of Exodus takes on a richer meaning. The liberation of the Israelites was not simply an escape from difficult labor but a moment that challenged the foundations of one of the most dominant societies in the ancient world.

This perspective also helps modern readers resist turning Exodus into something too small. The book is not merely about inspiration in hard times. It is about God acting within history against a system that seemed absolute. That does not make the story less personal. It makes it more powerful. The God who sees the suffering of Israel is not intimidated by the scale of the forces against them.

Why the Story Still Matters

By understanding the historical and cultural setting of Exodus, readers can better appreciate the significance of the events described in the narrative. The background of Egyptian power, religious belief, and social organization reveals why the confrontation between Moses and Pharaoh was so remarkable.

It also highlights why the deliverance of the Israelites became one of the defining moments in the history of their people and a story that would be remembered and retold for generations.

The story remains relevant because people continue to live inside systems that seem larger than they are. They still encounter forms of power that appear permanent, unquestionable, and deeply woven into the structure of daily life. Exodus reminds readers that no human system, however established, is ultimate.

No empire is beyond challenge. No ruler is beyond judgment. No people are beyond God's sight.

That does not mean every situation unfolds in the same way as the Exodus. It does mean the story continues to speak wherever human power presents itself as absolute and wherever people wonder whether deliverance is possible. The world behind the book may be ancient, but the questions raised by that world are still with us. Who truly rules? What powers can be trusted? Where does hope come from when systems seem too strong to confront?

Exodus answers those questions by telling a story in which the God of Israel steps into history and proves that the greatest strength in the world does not belong to an empire, but to Him.

Chapter 4

The Story or Flow of the Book

"Moses answered the people, 'Do not be afraid. Stand firm and you will see the deliverance the Lord will bring you today. The Egyptians you see today you will never see again. The Lord will fight for you; you need only to be still.'"
— Exodus 14:13–14

A Story That Unfolds in Stages

Exodus unfolds in clear stages. It begins with slavery in Egypt, moves through the rise of Moses and the confrontation with Pharaoh, and ends with the formation of Israel as a people shaped by covenant, worship, and God's presence. The book is not built around one isolated rescue event. It tells the story of a people moving from bondage to freedom and then learning what that freedom means.

The events of Exodus are connected. Each stage leads naturally to the next. Israel's suffering creates the need for rescue. Moses' story introduces the human leader through whom that rescue will come. Pharaoh's resistance drives the conflict forward. The plagues, the Passover, and the Red Sea mark the break from Egypt. The wilderness and Mount Sinai show that deliverance is only the beginning.

By the end of the book, the story has moved from forced labor under Pharaoh to covenant life under God. That is the flow of Exodus.

Israel's Oppression in Egypt

The story begins with Israel suffering under harsh labor in Egypt. Over time, the Israelites become numerous, and Pharaoh begins to see them as a threat. What had once been a place of provision in Joseph's day becomes a place of fear, control, and tyranny.

Pharaoh subjects the Israelites to forced labor and places them under taskmasters. They are used to build cities and strengthen the empire, but their lives are treated as expendable. Their days are marked by exhaustion, pressure, and the loss of freedom.

This is the world in which Exodus begins. Israel is not facing a minor hardship that can be fixed with small improvements. The people are trapped inside a system too powerful for them to escape on their own. The need is not relief alone. The need is rescue.

The Birth and Early Life of Moses

During this period of oppression, Moses is born. Pharaoh's fear of the Hebrews leads him to order the death of Hebrew male infants. In that setting, Moses survives because of the courage of others. His mother hides him, then places him in a basket along the Nile. Pharaoh's daughter finds him and raises him in the royal household.

The child marked for death is preserved inside the very house of power that sought to destroy him.

Moses grows up with access to Egyptian education, status, and privilege, yet he remains connected to his Hebrew identity. From the beginning, his life is marked by tension. He belongs near Pharaoh's court, but he is also tied to the people suffering beneath Pharaoh's rule.

Moses Between Two Worlds

As an adult, Moses becomes painfully aware of that tension. He sees an Egyptian beating a Hebrew laborer and responds by killing the Egyptian. When the act becomes known, Moses realizes he is no longer safe in Egypt. He flees into the wilderness of Midian.

That moment changes everything. Moses leaves behind the palace, the influence, and the world he has known. The man raised near power becomes an exile.

His first response to injustice is real, but it is not yet deliverance. He sees the problem, but he is not ready for the calling that lies ahead. Exodus slows down here and takes Moses into a long season of distance and reshaping.

Life in Exile

In Midian, Moses builds a different life. He becomes a shepherd, marries, and raises a family. The pace is quieter. The world of empire is behind him. His days are now shaped by wilderness, flocks, and ordinary responsibility.

These silent years matter. The man who once lived in Pharaoh's house is being formed in obscurity. He learns patience, endurance, and the rhythms of wilderness life. The future leader of Israel is not prepared in the spotlight, but in quiet faithfulness far from Egypt.

Then the stillness is interrupted.

The Burning Bush

While tending sheep near Horeb, Moses sees a bush that burns without being consumed. When he approaches, God speaks to him from the fire.

God tells Moses that He has seen the suffering of His people, heard their cries, and intends to bring them out of Egypt. Moses is commanded to return and confront Pharaoh.

This is the turning point. Until now, Israel's suffering has been clear, but God's action has remained mostly hidden. At the bush, the story changes. The God who has seen and heard now speaks and sends.

The mission will move through Moses, but the deliverance will come from God.

Moses' Calling and Hesitation

Moses does not respond with confidence. He hesitates. He questions his ability, his authority, and his speaking. He struggles to imagine how he could stand before Pharaoh and lead the Israelites out.

His hesitation is important because it shows what kind of leader he is. He is not introduced as fearless or self-assured. He is aware of his weakness and uncertain of himself. Yet God does not withdraw the calling. He promises His presence and gives Moses what he needs to obey.

So, Moses returns to Egypt.

The Confrontation with Pharaoh

The center of Exodus is the long confrontation between Moses and Pharaoh. Again and again, Moses delivers God's command: let the people go.

Pharaoh refuses. He will not surrender the labor force that strengthens Egypt. What follows is more than a political dispute. It is a conflict over authority. Pharaoh rules as if his power is absolute. Exodus is about to show otherwise.

The suffering of Israel has already been established. Now the question becomes clear: who truly rules?

The Plagues

In response to Pharaoh's refusal, a series of plagues strikes Egypt. Each one increases the pressure. Each one exposes the limits of Pharaoh's control. The empire that once looked unshakable begins to crack.

The plagues do not rush the story. They build tension. Pharaoh resists, the cost rises, and the difference between human power and divine authority becomes clearer with every stage.

For the Israelites, this would have been staggering. The system that had governed their lives for generations was being confronted in plain sight.

The Passover

The final plague leads to the Passover. The Israelites are given specific instructions for that night, and their obedience marks them out for protection. This moment becomes the threshold between slavery and freedom.

Passover is not only part of the escape story. It becomes part of Israel's memory. The people leave Egypt with a ritual that will remind future generations what God did for them.

Before they even depart, they are already being taught to remember.

The Exodus from Egypt

After the final plague, Pharaoh lets the Israelites go. The people gather what they can and leave the land where they have lived for generations. What once seemed impossible becomes real.

This is a moment of release, but also of rupture. Egypt has been the place of their suffering, yet it has also been the only world they know. They are free from slavery, but they are not yet settled into a new life. Freedom has begun, but it is still unfolding.

The Crossing of the Red Sea

Soon after, Pharaoh changes his mind and pursues them with his army. The Israelites find themselves trapped between the sea and the force they thought they had left behind.

Then comes one of the defining scenes in all of Scripture. The sea parts, Israel crosses on dry ground, and Pharaoh's army is stopped. What had seemed like a dead end becomes the path of escape.

This is the decisive break with Egypt. After the sea, the old life is behind them in a new and irreversible way. Pharaoh's grip is broken. The people are no longer merely leaving slavery. They have been brought out.

The Wilderness, Sinai, and a New Identity

The rest of Exodus shifts from escape to formation. The Israelites move through the wilderness toward Sinai, where they begin learning how to live as a free people under God's guidance.

At Sinai, they received the Ten Commandments and entered a covenant with God. They were also given instructions for the tabernacle, the visible sign that God would dwell among them.

By the end of the book, Exodus has become more than a rescue story. Israel has been delivered from oppression, but now must learn identity, worship, obedience, and community. The book begins with slavery in Egypt and ends with the beginnings of covenant life in God's presence.

That is the movement of Exodus. It starts in suffering, passes through confrontation and deliverance, and ends with a people being formed for a new way of life.

Chapter 5

Key Themes

"Now if you obey me fully and keep my covenant, then out of all nations you will be my treasured possession. Although the whole earth is mine, you will be for me a kingdom of priests and a holy nation."
— *Exodus 19:5–6*

Themes That Shape the Book

Several themes run throughout the book of Exodus, shaping the narrative and helping readers understand its fuller meaning. The events of the story are not simply historical episodes placed side by side. Instead, they form a connected narrative in which certain ideas frequently appear, guiding readers toward a deeper understanding of what the events represent and why they continue to matter.

These themes connect the different moments of the story and provide insight into how the experiences of the Israelites contribute to the larger message of the Bible. As the narrative unfolds, the story moves through moments of hardship, dramatic deliverance, and the gradual formation of a new identity for the people of Israel. Within these developments, certain ideas appear repeatedly, helping readers see the broader significance behind the events.

By paying attention to these themes, readers can better understand why the story of Exodus has remained so influential for generations. The themes found in the book do more than explain the past. They illuminate enduring truths about God, humanity, identity, worship, and the nature of faith. They also show that Exodus is not merely a record of what happened to one group of people long ago. It is a book that reveals how God acts, how people change, and how freedom becomes meaningful only when it is joined to purpose and relationship.

What makes Exodus especially powerful is that its themes do not remain isolated from one another. Deliverance leads to covenant. Covenant leads to law and guidance. Law and guidance shape identity. Identity is sustained through memory, worship, and the continued presence of God. And through all of it, faith is tested, stretched, and deepened. The themes of Exodus function less like separate topics and more like connected threads woven together into one larger message.

Deliverance

One of the most prominent themes in Exodus is deliverance. The entire narrative is built around the idea of rescue from slavery, beginning with the Israelites' suffering under forced labor in Egypt. For generations, the people have lived within a system that denies them freedom and subjects them to harsh conditions. Their lives are defined by demands they did not choose and by the authority of a ruler who sees them primarily as a resource rather than as human beings with dignity and worth.

Their cries for relief reflect the deep human longing for liberation from circumstances that seem impossible to escape. The Israelites find themselves trapped within a powerful empire that controls their labor and limits their future. Their suffering becomes the starting point of the story, highlighting the reality of injustice and hardship that many people experience throughout history. In this way, Exodus begins with a situation that is deeply human: a people in pain, waiting for something to change, uncertain whether anyone sees their condition or whether any hope remains.

When God responds to their suffering and begins the process of freeing them from Egypt, the story highlights the idea that deliverance is possible even when the situation appears overwhelming. The plagues, the confrontation with Pharaoh, and the crossing of the Red Sea all reinforce the message that the God of Israel has the power to intervene in human history. Deliverance in Exodus is not a vague spiritual idea detached from real life. It is concrete, visible, and disruptive. It changes political realities, overturns power structures, and opens the door to a future that once seemed unreachable.

These events demonstrate that the forces of oppression do not have the final word. The narrative shows that deliverance can arrive in unexpected ways and that circumstances that appear unchangeable can be transformed through divine action. At the same time, Exodus makes clear that deliverance is not only about escape. It is also about beginning again. The rescue of the Israelites is dramatic, but it is not the end of the story. It is the start of something new, something that will require growth, obedience, and trust.

This is part of what gives the theme of deliverance its lasting power. Readers are not only invited to admire the story of rescue but also to consider what rescue means. What does it look like when a people are brought out of bondage? What happens after the chains are broken? Exodus insists that deliverance is both a moment and a process. It begins with liberation, but it continues through transformation.

Covenant

Closely connected to the theme of deliverance is the idea of covenant. The story of Exodus does not end with the Israelites escaping from Egypt. Their liberation leads to something deeper: the establishment of a special relationship between God and His people. If the early chapters of the book focus on rescue, the later chapters show what that rescue is meant to create.

When the Israelites arrive at Mount Sinai, they enter into a covenant with God that defines their identity and purpose as a nation. This covenant represents a relationship built on commitment and trust. God promises to guide and protect the people, while the people agree to follow His instructions and live according to His ways. The covenant transforms the meaning of their deliverance. They are not simply a freed labor force wandering in the wilderness. They are a people entering into a relationship with the God who brought them out.

Through this covenant, the Israelites are not simply a group that has escaped slavery. They become a community shaped by a shared relationship with the God who delivered them. Their identity is no longer defined only by their past suffering but by the future that God is calling them to build. The covenant gives them belonging, purpose, and direction. It places their story within a larger framework and reminds them that their freedom is connected to a calling.

The covenant also establishes a sense of belonging and purpose. The people are invited to live in a way that reflects the character of the God they serve, creating a community built on justice, responsibility, and devotion. This is a crucial aspect of Exodus. The book does not portray freedom as independence from all obligation. Instead, it presents freedom as the opportunity to enter into the right kind of relationship. The Israelites are freed from Pharaoh in order to belong to God.

This theme matters because it shows that Exodus is not merely a story about breaking away from something oppressive. It is also a story about being bound to something life-giving. Covenant means that freedom is not empty. It is relational. It is purposeful. It is directed toward the formation of a people who reflect the presence, holiness, and character of the God who rescued them.

Law and Guidance

The theme of law and guidance also plays a central role in the narrative. As the Israelites move from slavery toward freedom, they must learn how to live as a people with shared responsibilities and moral direction. Leaving Egypt solves one problem, but it immediately raises another: how are these newly freed people supposed to live?

Life in Egypt required obedience to Pharaoh's authority, but it did not provide a framework for living as a free and unified community. Once the Israelites leave Egypt, they face the challenge of building a society that reflects new values and priorities. Freedom without guidance can become confusion, and liberation without moral direction can quickly unravel into disorder. Exodus recognizes this tension and addresses it directly.

The commandments given at Mount Sinai provide this framework. The Ten Commandments, along with additional instructions found later in Exodus, guide the people in their relationships with God and with one another. These teachings address issues such as worship, justice, honesty, rest, responsibility, and respect within the community. They are not random rules designed to control people for their own sake. They are instructions that help shape the lives of a people learning how to live well together.

Rather than functioning merely as rules, these laws establish the foundation for a society built on principles that reflect the character and intentions of God. They help the people understand how to use their freedom responsibly and how to create a community where justice and compassion can flourish. The law becomes part of the answer to a larger question raised by the book: what does life after deliverance look like?

The law also serves another important function. It teaches the people that holiness, justice, and worship are not separate categories. The way they treat one another is connected to the way they relate to God. Their public life, private conduct, and communal structures all matter. This means that freedom cannot be reduced to personal choice alone. It must also include communal responsibility and moral formation.

In this sense, law and guidance are not obstacles to freedom in Exodus. They are what make freedom sustainable. They give shape to the life of the community and help transform a group of former slaves into a people capable of living with order, purpose, and reverence.

God's Presence

Another significant theme in Exodus is the presence of God among His people. Throughout the story, God is not portrayed as distant or detached from the experiences of the Israelites. Instead, His presence is shown through various signs and actions that guide, protect, confront, and reassure them along their journey.

In Egypt, God demonstrates His power through the plagues that confront Pharaoh. In the wilderness, His presence appears in visible forms such as the pillar of cloud by day and the pillar of fire by night, which guide the Israelites as they travel. These signs remind the people that they are not alone in their journey and that their survival and direction do not depend solely on their own strength or wisdom.

One of the clearest symbols of God's presence is the tabernacle, the portable place of worship that the Israelites are instructed to build while they are in the wilderness. The tabernacle represents a place where God chooses to dwell among His people. This is one of the most striking ideas in Exodus. The God who defeated Pharaoh and displayed power over Egypt is also the God who chooses to be present among a wandering people in the wilderness.

This structure serves as a physical reminder that God's presence is not distant or abstract. Instead, it becomes a central part of the life of the community. Through the tabernacle, the narrative emphasizes that the relationship between God and Israel is lived out in daily life and shared worship. The people do not simply believe in a God who acted once in the past. They are called to live before a God who remains with them in the present.

The theme of divine presence is essential because it keeps the story from becoming merely historical or symbolic. The Israelites are not simply following a moral code or remembering a past rescue. They are learning to live with the reality that God is among them. His presence shapes their worship, their identity, and their understanding of where security truly comes from.

This helps explain why the tabernacle occupies so much space in the latter part of Exodus. To some modern readers, these chapters can feel highly detailed or repetitive. Yet their presence in the book makes an important theological point: the goal of deliverance is not only escape from bondage but life in the presence of God.

Faith and Trust

The journey through the wilderness introduces another recurring theme: faith and trust. Although the Israelites experience dramatic deliverance from Egypt, their journey toward becoming a nation is not without difficulty. In fact, many of their greatest struggles occur after the moment of liberation.

As they travel through unfamiliar territory and face challenges related to food, water, and uncertainty about the future, their faith is repeatedly tested. At various points, the people struggle with fear and doubt, questioning whether they can trust the God who brought them out of Egypt. They remember the security of the old life, even though it was a life of bondage, because uncertainty can make even oppression seem preferable to risk.

These moments reveal the tension that often exists between witnessing powerful acts of deliverance and maintaining trust during ongoing challenges. The Israelites must learn that faith is not limited to moments of dramatic rescue. Instead, it must also endure during seasons of waiting, confusion, and dependence. Trust is easy to speak about when the sea is parting; it becomes much harder when food is scarce, and the destination remains distant.

Through these experiences, the narrative shows that faith develops through the process of learning to rely on God even when circumstances remain uncertain. The wilderness journey becomes a place of spiritual growth, where the people gradually deepen their understanding of trust and dependence. This growth is not immediate, and it is certainly not smooth. It is marked by complaint, fear, failure, and repeated opportunities to learn.

Each challenge provides an opportunity for the Israelites to learn patience, humility, and perseverance. Over time, these lessons help shape the identity of the community. Faith in Exodus is not presented as a static possession but as something formed through movement, hardship, and experience. It is forged in the wilderness, where people must keep going without always knowing exactly how the future will unfold.

This makes the theme of faith especially relevant. Many readers recognize that trust is often hardest not at the beginning of a journey but in the middle, when the excitement of deliverance has faded, and the demands of daily dependence remain. Exodus speaks honestly into that reality.

Identity and Memory

Another central theme in Exodus involves the development of identity. When the story begins, the Israelites exist primarily as a group of laborers within Egyptian society. Their identity is defined largely by how others see them and by the roles they are forced to perform. They are known by their usefulness to an empire, not by the calling or dignity God intends for them.

Slavery has a way of shaping how people view themselves as well as how they are viewed by others. When individuals spend long periods of time within systems that limit their autonomy and restrict their opportunities, those systems can begin to influence how they understand their own value and purpose. The Israelites do not simply need to be moved out of Egypt geographically. They also need to be reshaped inwardly.

The process of leaving Egypt involves more than physical relocation. It also involves the gradual reshaping of how the Israelites understand themselves. As they travel through the wilderness, they begin to move from an identity imposed upon them by an empire toward an identity shaped by their relationship with God. This transition takes time. Identity does not change instantly simply because circumstances change. The habits, fears, and expectations developed under tyranny can linger even after the external structures of control have disappeared.

The wilderness journey becomes the environment where this deeper transformation takes place. During this time, the Israelites receive guidance, instruction, and experiences that slowly reshape how they see themselves and their place in the world. They are learning not only how to survive but also who they are.

The giving of the law at Mount Sinai plays a crucial role in this process. The commandments and instructions provided there offer the people a framework for understanding how their community should function. Rather than being governed by the arbitrary authority of Pharaoh, they are now invited to live according to principles that reflect justice, responsibility, and reverence for God. These teachings help form a shared identity rooted in common values. The people begin to understand themselves not merely as individuals who escaped bondage but as members of a community called to live in a particular way.

Closely related to identity is the theme of memory. Throughout the Bible, the events of the Exodus are remembered and retold repeatedly. The story becomes part of the collective memory of the people of Israel. This is important because memory is not simply about recalling facts. It is about preserving meaning. Communities are shaped by the stories they remember, the moments they repeat, and the events they treat as foundational.

The celebration of Passover illustrates this principle clearly. Each year, the people remember the night when they were delivered from Egypt. The ritual retelling of the story ensures that future generations understand the significance of what took place. By remembering the past, the people maintain a connection with the experiences that shaped their identity. Memory becomes a way of preserving meaning and reinforcing the values that guide the community.

This is one reason Exodus remains central within the Bible. It is not only a story of what happened once. It is a story meant to be remembered, retold, and lived from. The people become who they are in part by remembering what God has done.

The Themes That Shape the Message

Together, these themes—deliverance, covenant, law and guidance, God's presence, faith, identity, and memory—form the backbone of the message found in Exodus. Each theme contributes to the larger story of how God rescues His people and calls them into a new way of living.

Deliverance shows that oppression does not have the final word. Covenant reveals that God's rescue leads to relationship and purpose. Law and guidance provide the structure needed for a healthy community. God's presence assures the people that they are not alone in their journey. Faith reminds readers that trust often develops through difficult experiences. Identity shows that freedom must be lived into, not merely received. Memory preserves the meaning of what God has done and keeps future generations connected to the story that shaped them.

By following these themes throughout the book, readers gain a clearer understanding of how the experiences of the Israelites shape their identity and reveal the nature of the relationship between God and His people. Exodus is therefore much more than a historical account of national origins. It is a theological portrait of rescue, formation, and relationship. It shows how God acts in history, how people respond, and how freedom becomes meaningful when it is joined to worship, responsibility, and belonging.

The story of Exodus becomes more than a record of the past. It becomes a narrative that continues to speak to readers about freedom, responsibility, trust, identity, and the enduring presence of God in the midst of human struggle. That is why the book continues to matter. Its themes are ancient, but they are not outdated. They continue to illuminate the questions people still ask about suffering, deliverance, purpose, and what it means to live as people shaped by grace rather than bondage.

Chapter 6

Where People Get It Wrong

"They have been quick to turn away from what I commanded
them and have made themselves an idol cast in the shape of a calf.
They have bowed down to it and sacrificed to it and have said,
'These are your gods, Israel, who brought you up out of Egypt.'"
— Exodus 32:8

Misunderstanding the Message of Exodus

Some readers misunderstand the message of Exodus in a few
common ways. Because the story contains dramatic events such as
oppression, confrontation with political power, and the eventual
escape of an enslaved people, it can easily be interpreted through a
narrow lens that emphasizes only part of the narrative. These
scenes naturally capture attention. Pharaoh, plagues, deliverance,
and dramatic rescue are the kinds of moments that stay fixed in a
reader's mind. Yet when readers focus only on the surface
elements of the story, they can miss its deeper meaning.

This happens often with well-known biblical books. The
more familiar a story becomes, the easier it is to reduce it to a
handful of recognizable scenes or simplified lessons. Exodus is
especially vulnerable to this because its most dramatic moments
are so vivid. It is often remembered as a story of slavery, divine
judgment, and national escape, while the larger movement of the
book is overlooked. But Exodus is not merely a collection of
striking scenes. It is a carefully structured narrative with
theological depth, moral tension, and a clear movement from
bondage to covenant, from deliverance to worship, and from
rescue to responsibility.

The book of Exodus is not simply a historical record of events. It is a narrative shaped around theological and spiritual themes that reveal something about the nature of God, the identity of His people, and the process through which transformation takes place. When readers approach the story without recognizing these deeper themes, they may interpret the events in ways that overlook the broader purpose of the narrative. They may focus only on what the people were saved from while missing what they were saved for.

Another reason misunderstandings happen is that modern readers often bring their own assumptions to the text. People naturally read ancient stories through modern categories. They may emphasize psychology, politics, leadership, or activism because those are categories that feel familiar and immediate. While those approaches can highlight genuine aspects of the text, they can also narrow it. Exodus speaks into political realities, personal fear, social oppression, and leadership under pressure, but it never allows any one of those categories to define the story completely.

Recognizing common misunderstandings allows readers to approach Exodus with greater clarity. When the story is viewed within its full context, its message becomes richer and more meaningful. Rather than flattening the narrative into a single idea, readers begin to see how its different layers work together. The result is not only a better reading of Exodus itself but also a clearer understanding of how this book shapes the larger story of Scripture.

Reducing Exodus to a Political Story

One frequent mistake is treating the story primarily as a political liberation narrative. The events in Exodus clearly involve the escape of an oppressed people from the authority of a powerful empire, and this aspect of the story naturally draws attention.

Pharaoh represents a system of political and economic control, and the Israelites' departure from Egypt can easily be viewed as a dramatic example of resistance against an oppressive government.

Because of this, some readers interpret Exodus almost entirely in political terms. They see the narrative as a story about social revolution, national liberation, or resistance against political authority. In this interpretation, the focus remains on the struggle between the Israelites and the Egyptian empire, with Pharaoh serving as the primary antagonist and political freedom functioning as the main goal of the story.

There is some truth in this reading, but only in a limited sense. The book absolutely includes political realities. Pharaoh's rule is oppressive. The Israelites are economically exploited. The structures of Egyptian power are directly confronted and disrupted. Those elements are real and important. Yet when the political dimension becomes the whole story, something essential is lost.

While freedom from bondage is certainly a significant part of the narrative, the broader focus of the book lies elsewhere. Exodus consistently emphasizes the relationship between God and His people rather than simply the removal of political control. The conflict with Pharaoh is significant, but it is not the final destination of the story. Pharaoh is not merely a tyrant to be overthrown; he is also part of a larger narrative in which God reveals His power, His holiness, and His commitment to a people He intends to shape for His purposes.

This is why Exodus does not end at the Red Sea. If the point of the story were only liberation from political tyranny, the most natural conclusion would be the defeat of Pharaoh and the people's successful escape. But the book continues. It moves into the wilderness, to Sinai, to covenant, law, worship, and the tabernacle. These chapters make clear that Exodus is not only about leaving Egypt. It is about what kind of people Israel will become once Egypt is behind them.

To reduce Exodus to politics alone is to stop reading too early, even if one continues turning pages. The real center of the book lies not merely in the overthrow of oppression but in the formation of a people who belong to God.

This misunderstanding can also produce an unbalanced application of the book. If readers see Exodus only as a model for overthrowing unjust systems, they may miss its emphasis on holiness, obedience, worship, and communal responsibility. The narrative certainly affirms that God sees injustice and acts against it, but it also insists that rescue leads somewhere. It leads to a covenant. It leads to moral formation. It leads to life before God.

The political dimension is therefore real, but it is not ultimate. It is one part of a much larger story.

Freedom as the Beginning, Not the End

The liberation of the Israelites serves as the beginning of a new stage in their relationship with God, not merely the conclusion of their suffering. When the people leave Egypt, they do not simply disperse or begin forming a new political state. Instead, they move toward Mount Sinai, where they enter into a covenant with God that defines their identity and purpose as a community.

This moment reveals that the Exodus is about more than escape. The story moves beyond liberation and toward transformation. The Israelites are not only freed from slavery; they are invited into a new way of life centered on their relationship with God. This is one of the most impactful corrections a reader can make when approaching the book. Deliverance matters, but deliverance is not the endpoint. It is the doorway.

In this sense, the story of Exodus is not only about leaving something behind but also about moving toward something new. Deliverance opens the door to a closer relationship with God and a new understanding of what it means to live as His people. Freedom is therefore not portrayed as simple independence or self-determination. It is portrayed as belonging rightly. The Israelites leave the rule of Pharaoh in order to live under the guidance of God.

This changes the way the entire book is read. If freedom is the final goal, then the story ends with escape. But if the relationship is the goal, then the story continues through covenant, obedience, worship, and formation. The people are not delivered so that they can do whatever they want. They are delivered so that they can become who they were meant to be.

By focusing solely on the political dimension of the story, readers can miss the larger spiritual message that the narrative is intended to convey. Exodus insists that liberation without transformation is incomplete. The people must not only come out of Egypt; Egypt must, in a deeper sense, come out of them. Their habits, fears, and assumptions must be reshaped. They must learn to live not as slaves reacting to power, but as a covenant people responding to the presence of God.

This point is especially important for modern readers because freedom is often imagined primarily in negative terms, as freedom from restriction. Exodus adds a positive dimension. Freedom is also freedom for something. It is freedom for worship, for obedience, for justice, for shared life, and for right relationship with God. Without that positive dimension, the meaning of freedom remains thin.

Expecting Immediate Faithfulness

Another misunderstanding occurs when readers assume that the Israelites immediately became a faithful and unified nation after leaving Egypt. Because the dramatic moment of liberation often receives the most attention, it can be easy to imagine that the people responded with unwavering trust and obedience once they experienced God's deliverance.

From this perspective, the Exodus might appear as a turning point after which the Israelites consistently live with strong faith and clear devotion to God. The assumption seems natural enough. After all, they have seen plagues fall on Egypt, they have passed through the Red Sea, and they have witnessed the downfall of Pharaoh's army. It may seem reasonable to assume that such experiences would produce a stable and enduring faith.

However, the narrative itself presents a much more realistic picture of human behavior and spiritual growth. The book of Exodus does not portray the Israelites as instantly transformed heroes. Instead, it shows a community learning—sometimes slowly and imperfectly—how to live with freedom and responsibility. Their faith is real, but it is not mature. Their deliverance is dramatic, but their inner transformation unfolds gradually.

This honesty is one of the strengths of the book. Exodus does not idealize the people at the center of its story. It does not pretend that miraculous experiences automatically create moral or spiritual maturity. Instead, it shows that people can witness extraordinary acts of God and still struggle with fear, confusion, complaint, and resistance.

That makes the narrative far more believable and far more useful. Readers do not encounter a perfect people who instantly know how to live in freedom. They encounter a people who must be taught, corrected, and shaped over time. In that sense, the Israelites are not only ancient figures. They are mirrors of the reader's own condition—rescued, yet still learning; called, yet still uncertain; invited into faith, yet often slow to trust.

This misunderstanding often comes from assuming that a powerful experience should eliminate all future struggle. But Exodus shows that dramatic moments do not remove the need for formation. They may awaken faith, but they do not complete it. Growth still has to happen through repetition, testing, and response. The people still have to learn what it means to trust God in ordinary need, not just extraordinary rescue.

The Struggles of the Wilderness

In reality, the wilderness journey reveals many struggles and moments of doubt among the Israelites. As they travel away from Egypt and begin navigating unfamiliar territory, they encounter a variety of challenges that test their confidence and patience. The joy of escape quickly gives way to the realities of survival. The wilderness is not a place of instant stability. It is a place of exposure, dependence, and discomfort.

Concerns about food and water arise as the people move through difficult landscapes. The uncertainty of their destination creates anxiety about the future. At several points in the story, the Israelites express frustration and question whether leaving Egypt was the right decision. Their complaints reveal how quickly fear can reshape memory. Egypt, though a place of slavery, begins to appear in their minds as a place of predictability and provision.

These reactions may seem surprising given the dramatic miracles they have witnessed. Yet the narrative shows that witnessing powerful acts of deliverance does not automatically remove fear or doubt. Human beings often struggle to maintain trust even after experiencing moments of great hope. The memory of deliverance can be overwhelmed by the pressure of present discomfort. The challenge of the wilderness is not simply physical. It is spiritual and emotional as well.

These moments reveal that liberation does not automatically produce perfect faith or immediate stability. Instead, freedom exposes new kinds of weakness. In slavery, the structure of life is imposed from outside, however harshly. In freedom, people must learn how to think, act, trust, and live differently. That is a much greater challenge than simply changing location.

The wilderness becomes one of the most defining settings in the book, not because it is comfortable, but because it reveals the truth about the people. In the wilderness, their fears surface. Their expectations are tested. Their habits of dependence are exposed. The journey reveals not only where they are going but who they are.

It also reveals something about how God forms His people. He does not merely move them geographically. He leads them through situations that expose what is still unhealed, immature, or fearful within them. That process is uncomfortable, but it is necessary. Without it, the people might leave Egypt physically while still carrying Egypt's patterns within them.

Honest Portrait of Human Growth

The book of Exodus is remarkably honest about these struggles. Rather than presenting the Israelites as consistently faithful or heroic, the narrative acknowledges the tension that exists between witnessing dramatic acts of deliverance and maintaining trust over time. This honesty gives the book much of its power. It refuses to simplify the process of human growth.

The people often wrestle with fear and uncertainty as they attempt to understand what their new freedom means and how they should respond to the guidance they receive. Their reactions reflect the reality that spiritual growth and communal identity develop gradually rather than appearing instantly. They have been rescued, but they have not yet fully learned how to live as a rescued people.

In many ways, these struggles make the story more relatable. Readers see a community learning through experience rather than instantly becoming everything they are meant to be. That pattern is much closer to real life than a story of immediate transformation would be. People do not usually change all at once.

They grow in stages. They repeat mistakes. They hesitate. They resist. They learn slowly, often through hardship.

Exodus understands this. It portrays growth not as a straight line but as a difficult journey. There are moments of trust and worship, but also moments of fear and rebellion. The people move forward, but not without setbacks. This is not a flaw in the story. It is part of its truthfulness. Transformation is real, but it is rarely neat.

The honesty of Exodus also prevents readers from placing unrealistic expectations on themselves or others. It reminds them that spiritual maturity often develops over time and that struggle does not automatically mean failure. The important question is not whether the people have already become perfect, but whether they are being shaped through the process.

This realism also keeps readers from romanticizing either suffering or deliverance. Exodus does not present hardship as automatically noble, nor does it present rescue as automatically complete. Instead, it shows that God works with real people in real conditions, bringing them forward slowly, patiently, and persistently. That makes the book not only more honest but more hopeful.

Learning to Live in Freedom

The wilderness journey becomes a key part of the story because it reveals the process of learning to live as a free people. After generations of slavery, the Israelites must adjust to a completely different way of life. This adjustment is not merely logistical. It is moral, spiritual, and communal.

In Egypt, their lives were controlled by external authority. In the wilderness, they must learn to rely on God for provision, guidance, and direction. This transition requires patience, humility, and the willingness to grow through experience. It also requires the abandonment of certain ways of thinking formed under oppression. A people long shaped by fear do not immediately become a people shaped by trust.

The people must learn new patterns of trust, new habits of worship, and new ways of relating to one another as a community. They must learn that freedom includes responsibility. They must learn that a relationship with God affects every area of life, not just moments of crisis. They must learn how to remember what God has done, even when current circumstances feel uncertain.

This process includes moments of progress as well as moments of hesitation and doubt. Some days reveal growth. Others reveal how much remains to be learned. But this is exactly how real formation works. People are changed over time through repeated experiences of guidance, failure, correction, and renewal.

That is why the wilderness matters so much in Exodus. It is not just the setting between Egypt and Sinai. It is the place where freedom begins to be lived out. It is where the people discover that rescue is only the beginning. They are being taught how to become a different kind of community.

A common mistake is to treat the wilderness as a regrettable delay, as though the real story paused there. But Exodus presents it differently. The wilderness is not wasted space in the narrative. It is essential. Without the wilderness, there is no transition from rescued slaves to covenant people. It is the place where freedom is tested, stretched, and given substance.

The Slow Work of Transformation

By including these struggles in the narrative, the book presents a realistic portrayal of what transformation looks like. Freedom does not immediately eliminate every difficulty or create a perfectly ordered society. Instead, the journey toward becoming a faithful community involves learning, correction, and growth over time.

The Israelites' experiences in the wilderness illustrate how challenging it can be to move from a life shaped by injustice into a life shaped by covenant and responsibility. The transition requires both patience and perseverance as the people gradually discover what it means to live as God's people. This is not a one-time decision but an ongoing process.

The slow work of transformation is one of the deeper truths Exodus offers. Readers often want change to be immediate, decisive, and complete. But Exodus presents a more demanding and more believable picture. Real change usually unfolds through a series of tests, choices, setbacks, and lessons. It takes time for a people to learn how to live differently.

This slow process of transformation becomes a significant part of the message of Exodus. The book does not hide the difficulty of formation. It does not pretend that miracles remove the need for maturity. Instead, it shows that God's work in human lives often includes long stretches of shaping and preparation.

That makes the story both sobering and hopeful. Sobering, because it reminds readers that freedom carries demands and that change can be painful. Hopeful, because it shows that God does not abandon people simply because they are still learning. He continues to guide, instruct, and remain present even when the people are slow to trust.

This aspect of the book can also correct another misunderstanding: the idea that spiritual life should always feel clear and immediate if God is truly at work. Exodus suggests something more realistic. God may be most deeply at work in the very seasons that feel slow, demanding, or unfinished. The slowness of transformation is not evidence of His absence. Often, it is evidence of His patience.

Reading the Story Clearly

Recognizing these misunderstandings helps readers approach Exodus with a more balanced perspective. The story is not simply a political account of liberation, nor is it a narrative that portrays the Israelites as instantly transformed after they escaped from Egypt. It is neither flatter nor simpler than that.

Instead, Exodus is a complex and layered account that reveals how God rescues His people, establishes a covenant with them, and guides them through the difficult process of learning what it means to live in freedom. It is a story about deliverance, but also about identity. It is a story about power, but also about worship. It is a story about escape, but even more about formation.

By looking beyond the surface events and recognizing the underlying themes within the story, readers can better appreciate the richness of the narrative and the enduring message it continues to offer. They begin to see that Exodus is not only about what God did in the past but about how people are still shaped by freedom, responsibility, trust, and relationship with Him.

Reading the story clearly means refusing to reduce it. It means allowing its full weight to remain intact. When readers do that, Exodus becomes not only more understandable but more powerful. It reveals a God who does more than rescue people from bondage. He forms them into a people who can live in His presence.

And that may be the most significant correction of all. Exodus is not only about getting out. It is about being brought in—into covenant, into worship, into holiness, and into a life shaped by the nearness of God. When readers understand that the book becomes much larger than a rescue account. It becomes a defining vision of what redemption is meant to accomplish.

Chapter 7

What It Means for Modern Life

"But select capable men from all the people—men who fear God, trustworthy men who hate dishonest gain—and appoint them as officials over thousands, hundreds, fifties and tens."
— Exodus 18:21

Why Exodus Still Matters

Exodus still matters because it does more than preserve the memory of Israel's deliverance from Egypt. It gives readers a pattern for understanding how hardship, change, leadership, responsibility, and community unfold in real life. The book speaks not only to private faith but also to the lives of families, churches, organizations, and societies. It addresses what happens when people live under pressure, when leaders misuse power, when communities need courage, and when freedom must be learned rather than merely desired.

Although the events of Exodus took place in the ancient world, the issues it raises remain familiar. People still wrestle with injustice, fear, uncertainty, misuse of authority, personal limitation, and the longing for a life marked by dignity and purpose. Modern readers may not live under Pharaoh, but many understand what it feels like to face forces that seem larger than themselves. Those forces may appear in economic strain, public systems, personal crises, broken relationships, workplace constraints, or patterns of life that feel difficult to escape.

This is one reason Exodus continues to resonate. It is not trapped in its own historical moment. The story reflects conditions that reappear across generations. Communities still experience oppression and instability. Leaders still face the temptation to hold power for their own advantage. Individuals still find themselves in seasons where the future is unclear, and the way forward demands courage. Entire societies still struggle with the question of what justice, responsibility, and freedom should look like in practice.

Exodus also matters because it refuses shallow readings of life. It does not suggest that hardship is simple, that change happens overnight, or that freedom automatically solves every problem. The book is realistic about fear, suffering, resistance, and slow growth. Yet it is also realistic about hope. It shows that hardships are not always the end of the story, that leadership can emerge in weakness, and that a people can be reshaped even after long years of bondage.

Modern readers need that balance. They need a way to face what is broken without collapsing into despair, and a way to speak of hope without denying pain. Exodus does both. It names suffering clearly, but it also points toward renewal, order, and purpose. That is why the book continues to speak in both personal and public life.

Another reason Exodus remains powerful is that it speaks to both individual experience and shared life. Some biblical books are read mainly as private devotion, while others feel more obviously social or communal. Exodus reaches both levels at once. It tells the story of a suffering people, a resistant ruler, an unprepared leader, and a community learning how to live in freedom. That wide range makes it deeply useful for the present. It can help a person navigating fear, but it can also help a church, team, family, or community think more clearly about responsibility, leadership, moral order, and collective purpose.

In that sense, Exodus is not merely an ancient story to admire. It is a book that still speaks to modern questions about how people live, lead, endure, change, and build.

The Reality of Injustice and Struggle

One of the clearest ways Exodus speaks to modern life is by treating injustice seriously. The book begins with people living under a system that benefits from their labor while denying their dignity. Egypt grows stronger while Israel grows weaker. Power is arranged in a way that protects the empire and exploits the vulnerable. That pattern has appeared many times in human history and continues to appear in different forms today.

Modern societies may not mirror ancient Egypt in exact detail, but the underlying realities are still familiar. People continue to live under systems that are unfair, rigid, or difficult to challenge. Some endure economic structures that trap them in cycles of instability. Others live under social barriers that restrict opportunity. Others face manipulation, exploitation, or environments where their value is measured mainly by productivity rather than personhood. On a personal level, people also experience patterns of life that feel oppressive even when they are not political in form—circumstances where fear, strain, or dysfunction narrows their world.

Exodus does not pretend these realities are imaginary or insignificant. It does not tell suffering people to ignore what is happening. It does not ask them to rename injustice as a blessing. The suffering in Egypt is real, and the book treats it as real. That honesty is vital, because people are often pressured to minimize pain, move on too quickly, or pretend difficulty is less serious than it truly is.

At the same time, Exodus refuses to allow suffering to become the only lens through which reality is interpreted. It names injustice clearly, but it does not grant injustice final authority. Many people feel trapped not only by hardship itself, but by the belief that hardship is permanent. Exodus challenges that assumption. Systems of tyranny can appear immovable and still not have the last word.

This perspective helps readers do two things at once: tell the truth about what is wrong and refuse to believe that what is wrong is final. It guards against fatalism on one side and sentimentality on the other. Exodus does not glorify oppression, romanticize suffering, or imply that pain is good in itself. The evil of Egypt remains evil. But the story also shows that evil does not control the whole future.

Modern life requires that kind of clarity. People must learn to name injustice without being defined by it and pursue renewal without denying reality.

Transformation Often Begins in Difficulty

Exodus also shows that transformation often begins before circumstances improve. The Israelites do not begin their journey from a place of strength, control, or readiness. Their story begins in hardship. Moses is called while the problem is still active. Pharaoh has not softened. The people are not yet free. The burden remains real.

Many people assume meaningful change can only begin once they feel strong enough, secure enough, or clear enough. They wait for ideal conditions. They imagine transformation starts after fear has lifted, after confusion has passed, or after every resource is in place. Exodus shows a different pattern. Change often begins while weakness is still present and while the situation remains unresolved.

This happens across many areas of life. A person may begin healing while grief is still sharp. A family may begin rebuilding while trust is still fragile. A leader may begin responding responsibly while answers are incomplete. A community may begin moving toward justice while obstacles still remain. In each case, the beginning does not wait for perfect conditions.

Exodus shows that what looks like the worst place to begin may actually be the place where beginning becomes possible.

Suffering in Egypt is not good, but it becomes the setting in which the cry for deliverance rises. Moses' uncertainty is not strength, but it becomes the place where calling meets obedience. The path does not open after weakness disappears. It opens in the middle of dependence.

For modern readers, this removes two common excuses: waiting for perfect readiness and assuming fear disqualifies action. Exodus shows that people can begin while still uncertain, respond while still afraid, and move while still carrying limitations.

Difficulty alone does not transform anyone. But difficulty can expose what matters, strip away illusion, and create space for a different kind of dependence. Renewal is not always born from comfort. Many times, it begins in the place people would rather escape.

That lesson cuts against a culture shaped by immediacy and performance. Modern life rewards polish, speed, and visible momentum. Exodus values something different. It values faithful movement even when the beginning looks small, uncertain, and unimpressive.

The First Steps Toward Change

Because Exodus understands how transformation begins, it also shows what the first steps look like. Change rarely begins with a complete plan. More often, it begins with a response. Someone tells the truth. Someone accepts responsibility. Someone obeys before the outcome is visible. Someone stops pretending the situation is manageable and begins moving in the direction of what is right.

Moses embodies this pattern. When he is called, he does not step forward with polished confidence. He hesitates. He questions his ability. He sees the size of the task and knows he cannot accomplish it alone. Yet he goes. That movement matters. The larger deliverance that follows does not begin with Moses feeling ready. It begins with Moses responding.

In modern life, people often feel paralyzed because they cannot see the entire future. They want certainty before obedience. They want guarantees before action. They want a complete map before taking the first step. Exodus challenges that instinct. Progress often begins before clarity arrives.

The first step toward change may be confronting a harmful pattern, speaking honestly in a strained relationship, seeking counsel, setting a boundary, asking forgiveness, or admitting that a strategy is failing. Sometimes it means stepping into leadership or initiating a difficult conversation that has been avoided for too long.

These first steps may appear small, but they matter. A first step changes direction. It interrupts inertia. It opens the possibility that what seemed fixed might not remain so.

For people who feel stuck, Exodus offers a clear reminder: not seeing the end does not mean no beginning is possible.

Freedom Brings Responsibility

Another significant lesson Exodus offers modern readers is that freedom is not self-sustaining. Deliverance is important, but what follows deliverance is just as important. The Israelites do not leave Egypt and instantly become a stable, wise, and unified people. Their departure from oppression is only the beginning of a much longer process. Once they are free, they must learn how to live as people who are no longer defined by Pharaoh's control.

That transition proves difficult. Habits formed under slavery do not disappear overnight. The people carry old fears, old assumptions, and old patterns of thinking with them into the wilderness. Even after deliverance, they sometimes react as though Egypt still governs their future. They struggle to trust provision. They question leadership. They remember the past selectively and sometimes even begin to romanticize the very place that once enslaved them.

This part of the story speaks directly to modern life. Many people long for freedom from difficult circumstances—freedom from harmful environments, destructive patterns, or burdens that have weighed heavily on their lives. Yet the moment freedom arrives, a new challenge begins. The question shifts from *How do I escape?* to *How do I live now that I am free?*

Freedom without formation can easily collapse into confusion.

The Israelites must learn how to live as a people who are no longer slaves. That means learning responsibility. They must begin to organize their community differently. They must learn new rhythms of worship, new patterns of trust, and new ways of relating to one another. Deliverance creates opportunity, but opportunity must still be shaped into a life that is ordered and meaningful.

Modern readers face the same challenge. A person who leaves a destructive environment still must decide how they will live moving forward. A community that gains freedom from injustice still must build systems that protect dignity and promote fairness. A family that survives a difficult season still must choose the values and habits that will guide their future.

Freedom, in other words, creates responsibility.

Exodus teaches that liberation is not simply the removal of constraint. It is the beginning of a new kind of life that must be learned. The people are not only freed *from* Egypt; they are being formed *for* something greater.

Without direction and purpose, freedom can quickly become disorientation. People who escape old patterns may unintentionally recreate them in new forms if they do not learn new ways of living. The wilderness becomes the place where those lessons begin.

Learning to Live with Purpose

Closely connected to responsibility is the question of purpose. The Israelites are not delivered merely so they can wander without direction. Their freedom is tied to covenant, worship, and a new communal identity. They are being formed into a people who will live differently because they now belong to God and to one another in a new way.

Purpose provides direction for freedom.

Without purpose, people often drift. They may achieve the change they once prayed for, only to discover that they are unsure how to build a life around it. Relief from one burden simply reveals deeper questions about meaning, calling, and responsibility.

Many modern readers know this experience well. Someone may work for years toward a goal—a new career, a restored relationship, a hard-earned opportunity—only to discover that achieving the goal does not automatically answer the question of what comes next. The removal of pressure creates space for a new question: *What kind of life will I build now?*

Exodus refuses to leave that question unanswered. The giving of the law at Sinai marks a crucial turning point in the story. The people are taught how justice should function, how worship should order their lives, and how relationships within the community should be shaped. These instructions do not exist to restrict freedom but to guide it.

Purpose protects freedom from dissolving into chaos.

When people understand what they are living for, they can endure challenges more steadily. They can make decisions with greater clarity. They can build communities that reflect shared values rather than momentary impulses. Purpose gives direction to movement.

This is one reason Exodus continues to resonate today. The story invites readers to consider not only what they have been delivered from, but also what they are being called toward. Freedom opens the door to responsibility, and responsibility opens the door to purpose.

Leadership in Times of Uncertainty

Exodus also offers a profound reflection on leadership. The book does not present leadership as something reserved for the confident, the charismatic, or the naturally impressive. Moses himself begins the story reluctant and uncertain. He questions his ability to speak. He doubts his capacity to lead. He worries about how others will respond to him.

Yet Moses becomes the central human leader in the story.

This reveals something significant about how leadership often develops. Leadership is not always the result of natural confidence. More often, it grows out of obedience, persistence, and willingness to carry responsibility even when the path forward is unclear.

Modern culture frequently celebrates a very different image of leadership. Leaders are often expected to appear decisive, self-assured, and fully in control. While confidence can be helpful, Exodus suggests that character and humility matter more. Humility, endurance, teachability, and dependence on God often prove far more important than outward charisma.

Moses repeatedly faces moments when the situation feels overwhelming. The people complain. Pharaoh resists. The wilderness stretches on longer than expected. Yet leadership in Exodus does not mean possessing every answer. It means continuing to respond faithfully even when the outcome remains uncertain.

This perspective can be freeing for many modern readers. People who feel unprepared for responsibility often assume that their uncertainty disqualifies them from leadership. Exodus offers a different picture. Leadership may grow precisely in those who recognize their own limitations and therefore depend more deeply on God.

The story also reminds readers that leadership is rarely a solitary effort. Moses receives help from others, including Aaron and, later, the wise counsel of Jethro. Responsibility is shared. Burdens are distributed. Leadership becomes a collaborative effort rather than the task of one individual carrying everything alone.

In modern communities, this lesson remains essential. Healthy leadership recognizes the value of cooperation, accountability, and shared responsibility. No single person carries the whole weight of the journey.

The Role of Community

Another central theme in Exodus is the importance of community. The story is not primarily about one individual achieving personal freedom. It is about a people leaving bondage together and learning how to live together afterward.

This collective dimension shapes nearly every part of the narrative. The people travel together, struggle together, receive instruction together, and worship together. Their future is tied not only to personal decisions but to the health of the community as a whole.

Modern culture often emphasizes individual achievement and personal autonomy. While individual responsibility remains relevant, Exodus reminds readers that many aspects of life are deeply communal. Families, churches, organizations, and societies are shaped by how well people learn to live with shared responsibility.

Communities must learn how to support one another during times of uncertainty. They must develop habits of trust, honesty, and mutual care. They must build structures that allow people to flourish together rather than compete against one another for survival.

The Israelites' journey demonstrates how challenging this process can be. Conflicts arise. Complaints surface. The community must repeatedly learn how to move forward despite disagreement and fear. Yet through those struggles, a shared identity slowly begins to form.

Modern readers may see echoes of this process in their own communities. Organizations navigating change must learn to adapt together. Families moving through difficult seasons must support one another with patience and grace. Churches seeking renewal must rediscover practices that strengthen unity and purpose.

Exodus reminds readers that freedom is not merely personal. It is relational. A people who learns to live well together create the conditions for a healthier future.

Living Exodus Today

Taken together, these themes explain why Exodus remains so relevant for modern life. The book provides more than historical insight. It offers a framework for thinking about hardship, leadership, responsibility, and hope.

It teaches readers that injustice should be named honestly, but not allowed to define the future. It shows that transformation often begins in difficult circumstances rather than comfortable ones. It reminds people that the first step toward change is often simple obedience rather than complete understanding.

Exodus also teaches that freedom must be shaped by responsibility and guided by purpose. Leadership grows through humility and endurance. Communities flourish when people learn to carry burdens together.

Perhaps most importantly, the story encourages readers to take a longer view of life. Modern culture often prioritizes immediate results and quick solutions. Exodus reveals a different rhythm. Change unfolds gradually. Growth requires patience. The most significant developments often occur beneath the surface long before they become visible.

This longer perspective can steady readers during uncertain seasons. When the path forward feels unclear, Exodus reminds them that meaningful transformation rarely happens overnight. The journey may be longer than expected, but that does not mean it lacks direction.

In the end, Exodus remains powerful because it tells the truth about both hardship and hope. It acknowledges the reality of struggle without surrendering to despair. It recognizes the complexity of human weakness while pointing toward the possibility of renewal.

For modern readers seeking guidance in a complicated world, that combination remains deeply valuable. The story invites them to see their own lives within a larger narrative—one in which hardship does not have the final word, and where even difficult journeys can lead toward freedom, purpose, and renewed community.

Chapter 8

Modern Reflection

"When Pharaoh let the people go, God did not lead them on the road through the Philistine country, though that was shorter. For God said, 'If they face war, they might change their minds and return to Egypt.' So God led the people around by the desert road toward the Red Sea. The Israelites went up out of Egypt ready for battle."
— Exodus 13:17–18

Seeing Ourselves in the Story

Exodus continues to speak with unusual power because it does not remain safely distant from the reader. The story has a way of drawing people in until they begin to recognize themselves somewhere within it. They may not stand under Pharaoh's rule, walk through the Red Sea, or camp in the wilderness of Sinai, yet the inward movement of the book feels deeply familiar. Readers know what it is like to feel trapped, to long for change, to fear the unknown, to question the path ahead, and to wonder whether God is still present in the middle of uncertainty.

That is one reason the book has endured. Stories continue across centuries when they capture something true about the human heart. Exodus does this with unusual clarity. Beneath the historical details lies a pattern of experience that readers still recognize: oppression, longing, rescue, uncertainty, testing, waiting, and gradual formation. The outer landscape belongs to the ancient world, but the inner landscape remains painfully current.

Many people come to Exodus carrying their own version of Egypt. For some, it is a season of grief that has narrowed life and made joy feel far away. For others, it is fear, shame, exhaustion, unresolved pain, or a pattern that has quietly mastered them for years. For others still, it is an outward circumstance that seems impossible to change—a strained relationship, a confusing responsibility, a season of loss, or a future that feels closed in. The details vary, but the experience is recognizable: something has become oppressive, and the soul begins to cry for relief.

Exodus gives language to that condition. It assures readers that they are not the first to live under pressure or to wonder whether freedom is possible. It also gives them permission to see their lives as a journey rather than a single fixed moment. Many people judge themselves harshly because their present season feels unfinished. They assume that if life still feels uncertain, something must already be wrong. Exodus gently challenges that instinct. Unfinished does not mean abandoned, and in-between does not mean lost.

Much of life unfolds this way. A person may still be becoming. A hard season may still be unfolding toward a meaning that cannot yet be seen. A long road may still be shaping a life in ways that will only become clear later. Exodus leaves room for that slower, humbler way of seeing.

The story, therefore, becomes more than an account of what happened to Israel. It becomes a mirror. It quietly asks readers where they might be in the journey. Are they still under a weight that has not yet broken? Are they standing on the edge of change and afraid to move? Are they in a wilderness season where the old life is behind them, but the new one has not fully formed? Or are they beginning to suspect that what once felt like delay may have been preparation all along?

These questions move beyond the interpretation of the text. They touch the soul itself. That is part of why Exodus continues to speak so directly. It offers a way to read not only Scripture, but also the unfolding story of one's own life.

The Meaning of the Wilderness

For many readers, the deepest point of connection comes in the wilderness. The wilderness in Exodus is not simply a stretch of geography between Egypt and the promised land. It is the place where the people live between what was and what will be. They have left bondage, but they have not yet entered rest. The old life has ended, but the new life has not fully settled. That in-between space becomes the setting where much of the real formation happens.

Perhaps that is why the wilderness still feels so familiar.

Many people recognize the feeling immediately. They know what it is like to leave something behind without yet knowing what will replace it. They know the unease of standing in a season where the future has not taken shape and where familiar supports no longer hold the same weight they once did. Life in those moments can feel exposed, quiet, and unsettled.

The wilderness carries a particular kind of discomfort because it strips away illusion. In more stable seasons, people often rely on routines, structures, titles, relationships, momentum, or visible progress to reassure themselves that life is under control. But wilderness seasons reduce those supports. What remains is not only external uncertainty, but the revealing question of what a person actually trusts when the usual supports disappear.

That exposure can feel severe. It may reveal previously hidden fears, attachments that are stronger than expected, and hopes that have become fragile. Yet Exodus suggests that this exposure is not meaningless. The wilderness is not only the place where people feel weak. It is also the place where deeper formation quietly becomes possible.

In the story, the Israelites do not move straight from rescue into comfort. They move into dependence. The wilderness becomes the environment in which they begin learning what freedom means, what trust requires, and how identity slowly changes over time. They are no longer under Pharaoh, but they are not yet settled in maturity. The drama has moved from the outside to the inside.

Modern readers often find themselves in similar terrain. They may be in a season after loss, after upheaval, after change, after crisis, or after leaving something that once defined them. They are no longer where they were, but they are not yet where they expected to be. Exodus offers a name for that experience. Barren places may still be holy places. Seasons of uncertainty may still carry hidden purpose.

Living Between Two Stages

To live between two stages is one of the more difficult human experiences. Something old has ended or begun to end, but what is new has not yet arrived with clarity. A person may have stepped away from a former role, identity, habit, or expectation and still feel unsure of who they are becoming. The transition may be necessary, but it rarely feels comfortable.

Exodus understands that tension. The people leave Egypt, but they do not immediately become the people they are meant to be. They carry memories from the old life into the new terrain. They are physically out, but inwardly, much is still unsettled. Their reactions reveal how deeply the old patterns remain.

That is often how transition works for readers as well. People can leave an old chapter and still carry its emotional habits into the next one. They may be free from an external pressure while still thinking like someone who lives under it. They may be offered a new beginning while still feeling inwardly tied to old fears. Change may be real, yet the soul takes longer to arrive.

Living between stages can create a strong temptation to rush. People want an immediate resolution. They want quick proof that the path they are on is correct. They want reassurance that the cost of leaving the old life behind will be worth it. Exodus rarely grants that kind of closure on demand. Instead, it shows people learning through movement. They learn by walking. They learn through provision, correction, waiting, failure, memory, and repeated dependence.

Being between stages does not mean being without direction.

A person may still be in a middle chapter and yet remain fully within God's care. The unfinished season may still belong to Him. The absence of immediate clarity does not mean the journey has lost its meaning.

Many readers feel relief the moment they recognize this. Much of life unfolds in movement rather than arrival. The space between endings and beginnings may be exactly where lasting wisdom is learned.

The Emotional Reality of Transition

One of the reasons Exodus feels so honest is that it does not hide the emotional complexity of change. The Israelites do not move through the wilderness with uninterrupted confidence. They worry about food, water, safety, direction, and survival. They complain. They fear. They remember Egypt with distorted nostalgia. They become impatient. Their emotions move in conflicting directions because that is what real transition often feels like.

Many readers recognize that mixture immediately. A person can be moving in the right direction and still feel anxious, weary, frustrated, and emotionally divided. They may know they should not go back, yet still miss what was familiar. They may be grateful and exhausted at the same time. They may trust and tremble within the same season.

Exodus leaves space for that honesty.

It does not portray change as effortless or emotionally clean. Even necessary transitions can involve grief. People often mourn what they are leaving behind, even when what they are leaving was painful. The known world, however difficult, carries a kind of predictability. The unknown future asks for a different kind of courage.

For many readers, recognizing this brings a quiet sense of relief. Emotional struggle does not place them outside the life of faith. Fear, fatigue, frustration, and hesitation often accompany real change. They are not always signs of failure. Sometimes they are simply signs that a real road is being walked.

Exodus does not celebrate unbelief or glorify complaint. Yet it does show that God's people are often more mixed, frail, and unsettled than they wish they were. That honesty makes the story credible. It tells the truth about what it feels like to move through uncertainty without pretending the emotional cost is small.

For readers in transition, that honesty can feel like mercy. It allows them to stop performing strength they do not actually feel and to bring their real condition before God.

Facing Change in Modern Life

When readers carry the story of Exodus into their own time, they often begin to recognize how many wilderness-shaped seasons still exist in ordinary life. The details may look different from the ancient journey through Sinai, but the inward experience is strikingly similar. Seasons of illness, grief, family disruption, spiritual dryness, unexpected responsibility, disappointment, or difficult decisions can place a person in terrain that feels unfamiliar and uncertain.

Life can shift quickly. What once felt stable can become unsettled almost overnight. Roles change. Plans unravel. Relationships grow strained. The future that once seemed clear can become difficult to read. In those moments, people often find themselves asking questions very similar to those raised in the wilderness.

Am I on the right path?

Why does this feel harder than I expected?

Why is clarity taking so long?

Why does the past still pull at me?

Why does the future feel so undefined?

Questions like these reach beyond practical concerns. They touch identity, trust, and endurance. They force a person to confront what they truly believe about God, about themselves, and about the meaning of the road they are walking.

Exodus does not provide quick answers to every such question. Instead, it offers something quieter but often more helpful. It offers a way to live faithfully while those questions remain open. The story shows that uncertainty does not always interrupt growth. Sometimes it becomes the very place where growth happens most deeply.

Modern culture often struggles to recognize this. Many people are trained to expect quick results, measurable progress, and visible signs that life is moving forward. When those signs disappear, discouragement quickly follows. Waiting begins to feel like failure. Slowness begins to feel like a mistake.

Exodus presents a very different rhythm. The story moves forward, but it does not move quickly. The people walk, stop, struggle, learn, fail, and begin again. Much of what is happening inside them cannot be measured in the moment. Only later does it become clear that the wilderness was not simply wasted time.

Readers who are living through their own uncertain seasons may find comfort in that slower rhythm. A hard season may not look impressive from the outside. It may appear quiet, repetitive, or even stagnant. Days may feel filled with waiting, prayer, confusion, or endurance rather than visible achievement.

Yet those very conditions may be shaping something that easier seasons rarely produce. Patience may be deepening.

Illusions of control may be loosening. Dependence on God may be growing more honest. A person may be learning to live with less entitlement and greater humility. These changes are rarely dramatic, but they are often lasting.

Exodus does not pretend that difficulty is pleasant. The wilderness is still difficult terrain. But the story suggests that difficulty is not always empty. Sometimes more is happening in those barren places than the traveler can yet see.

Reflecting on Our Own Journeys

Because of this, Exodus gently invites readers into reflection. The story encourages them to consider not only what they are going through, but who they are becoming while they go through it.

That question can feel uncomfortable. Many people measure life primarily by external markers such as success, productivity, comfort, or stability. When those markers disappear, it becomes easy to assume that life itself has lost direction.

Exodus shifts the focus. It turns attention toward slower questions.

What is this season revealing about my fears?

What do I reach for when certainty disappears?

What am I tempted to control that I cannot truly control?

Where am I resisting what God may be trying to form in me?

Am I becoming more patient, more honest, more dependent on God?

Or am I only trying to escape the discomfort as quickly as possible?

Questions like these are rarely easy, but they often lead to greater clarity. The wilderness in Exodus is not only a place of external challenge. It is also a place of internal revelation. As the Israelites travel through it, their reactions begin to uncover what truly shapes them. Their fears, desires, loyalties, and assumptions slowly come to the surface.

In much the same way, difficult seasons often reveal things that remain hidden during more comfortable periods. A person may discover attachments they did not know they carried. They may notice habits of thought that quietly governed their decisions. They may realize that certain forms of security mattered more to them than they previously admitted.

Reflection does not remove the difficulty of the journey, but it can give the journey meaning. Instead of viewing the wilderness only as a place to escape, readers may begin to see it as a place where deeper truths are being revealed.

Sometimes that realization comes slowly. Many people do not understand the significance of a difficult season while they are still inside it. Insight often arrives later, when the distance of time allows them to see what was forming beneath the surface.

Exodus acknowledges this limitation. The Israelites themselves rarely understand the full meaning of what is happening while they are living through it. They are simply asked to keep walking, to keep trusting, and to keep responding to the guidance they receive.

Readers today often find themselves in the same position. They may not know exactly what God is accomplishing in a particular season. Yet they are still invited to practice faithfulness in the next step that lies before them.

Growth in the Wilderness

One of the quiet encouragements in Exodus is that the wilderness is not wasted ground. What appears to be a delay gradually becomes a formation. What feels unstable begins to shape a different kind of strength.

This transformation does not happen instantly. The Israelites struggle repeatedly. They complain, doubt, and misunderstand. Yet the wilderness continues to teach them. Through provision, correction, and memory, they slowly begin to change.

Over time, their identity becomes clearer. They are no longer simply slaves reacting to years of harsh rule. They are being formed into a people who will live with covenant, worship, and shared responsibility at the center of their lives.

That process matters. It shows that pain is not the only thing taking place in painful seasons. Hardship remains hardship, but it may also become the environment where endurance grows, and vision deepens.

Many readers eventually recognize a similar pattern in their own lives. A season that once felt like wandering may later appear as preparation. A loss that once seemed only destructive may reveal how certain illusions were broken. A delay that once caused frustration may later appear as the necessary space where meaningful work could take place.

This recognition rarely happens immediately. Often it appears only in hindsight. Yet when it does appear, it can reshape how a person understands their own story. Instead of seeing the wilderness as a meaningless interruption, they may begin to see it as part of a larger movement of formation. Exodus honors that slower understanding. It recognizes that people often do not see the significance of a season until they have already passed through it.

Encouragement During Transition

For those currently living in uncertain seasons, Exodus offers a steady kind of encouragement. It reminds readers that confusion does not necessarily mean failure, and delay does not necessarily mean abandonment.

A process may still be unfolding even when its direction is not immediately obvious. Progress may still be real before it becomes visible. This perspective can help people endure without demanding immediate explanation. It allows them to move at the pace of formation rather than the pace of anxiety.

In a culture that values speed and constant movement, that slower rhythm can feel unfamiliar. Many people are accustomed to interpreting life quickly. They expect answers, conclusions, and clarity as soon as possible.

Exodus gently challenges that expectation. The story suggests that some of the most important work in life happens quietly and gradually. Growth may remain hidden for long stretches of time. What feels delayed may actually be developing.

The wilderness does not always produce immediate clarity, but it can produce depth.

It can deepen patience.

It can strengthen trust.

It can loosen attachments that once controlled a person's sense of security.

It can teach someone to rely on God in ways that were only theoretical before.

None of these developments happens instantly. Yet over time, they can reshape a life in ways that more comfortable seasons rarely accomplish.

A Story That Continues to Speak

This is one reason Exodus continues to speak so powerfully across generations. The book does not merely describe ancient events. It captures the rhythms of real human experience.

People still encounter seasons of bondage and seasons of freedom. They still walk through moments of rescue and moments of confusion. They still experience waiting, testing, and gradual formation.

Exodus gives language to those movements. It helps readers see that their own stories may contain similar patterns. What feels like wandering may later be recognized as instruction. What feels like disruption may later be understood as redirection. What feels like loss may later become preparation.

The story encourages readers to hold their lives with patience. It reminds them that unfinished chapters are still chapters, and unclear ground may still be holy ground.

Above all, Exodus points to the presence of God within those uncertain seasons. The Israelites were not abandoned in the wilderness, even when they felt lost or afraid. Their journey remained under God's care, even when they could not see the full direction ahead.

That same reassurance continues to echo for modern readers. The wilderness may feel lonely, but it is not empty. The road may feel uncertain, but it is not meaningless.

God meets His people not only at the destination, but also along the long middle stretches of the journey.

And often it is in those middle places—where certainty fades, and dependence grows—that the deepest transformation quietly begins.

Chapter 9

Reflection Questions

*"Commemorate this day, the day you came out of Egypt, out of
the land of slavery, because the Lord brought you out of it with a
mighty hand."*
— Exodus 13:3

What Does Freedom Mean in Your Own Life?

Freedom can be understood in many different ways depending on
a person's experiences, circumstances, and values. For some
individuals, freedom may involve independence from external
pressures such as financial hardship, social expectations, unhealthy
relationships, or difficult environments. Others may associate
freedom with the ability to pursue meaningful goals, make
decisions without fear of retaliation, or live according to deeply
held beliefs and convictions. The meaning of freedom is rarely
one-dimensional. It often includes emotional, spiritual, relational,
and practical aspects that shape the way a person understands
their life.

The concept of freedom can also shift over time. What a
person once viewed as freedom during one stage of life may look
different during another. Early in life, freedom may mean
independence, movement, opportunity, or the ability to choose
one's own direction. Later, it may involve the ability to live with
purpose, maintain meaningful relationships, serve others well, or
contribute to something greater than oneself. In some seasons,
freedom may feel like release from something painful. In others, it
may feel like the ability to fully step into a calling or responsibility.

This question matters because people often define freedom too narrowly. It is easy to think only in terms of what one wants to escape. Yet Exodus reminds readers that freedom is not simply about what people are freed from. It is also about what they are freed for. The Israelites were not merely released from Egypt so they could drift without purpose. Their deliverance led them toward covenant, identity, worship, and responsibility. Their freedom opened space for a different way of living.

Reflecting on the concept of freedom invites readers to think more carefully about their own lives. What burdens, fears, or limitations have shaped their sense of what freedom means? What opportunities or responsibilities have emerged as a result of changes they have already experienced? What kind of life becomes possible when fear, limitation, or bondage no longer has the final word?

This question encourages readers to examine how they define freedom in their own lives and how that freedom shapes the decisions they make moving forward. It also creates space to ask whether the freedom they seek is merely freedom from discomfort, or whether it is connected to a deeper purpose, identity, and way of living.

This reflection can become even more meaningful when readers ask what currently holds the most power over them. For some, the answer may involve outside circumstances. For others, it may involve internal patterns such as fear, resentment, shame, passivity, or the need for approval. In that sense, freedom is not always about geography or opportunity. Sometimes it is about the slow release from habits of mind and heart that have quietly shaped a person's life for years.

Exodus gives readers language for that kind of reflection. It reminds them that leaving oppression is only one part of the journey. The fuller question is whether they are learning how to live in the kind of freedom that leads to stability, integrity, and purpose. Freedom that lacks direction can become empty.

Freedom joined to truth, and responsibility can become the beginning of a more whole life.

What Challenges Often Accompany Major Life Changes?

Major life changes rarely occur without difficulty. Transitions such as moving to a new place, beginning a new career, ending a long-standing chapter of life, facing unexpected circumstances, or entering unfamiliar responsibilities often bring uncertainty and emotional strain. Even when change is positive, it can still be disruptive. New opportunities may bring excitement, but they also require adjustment, patience, and the willingness to let go of what is familiar.

Even positive changes can feel overwhelming because they require individuals to leave behind routines, identities, and assumptions that once gave structure to daily life. The process of adapting to unfamiliar environments or responsibilities can create feelings of doubt, hesitation, or anxiety. People may question whether they made the right decision, whether they are prepared for what lies ahead, or whether they will be able to handle the demands of their new circumstances.

The story of the Israelites leaving Egypt illustrates this reality clearly. Their departure from slavery represents a moment of liberation, yet the journey that follows introduces new challenges. The people must learn how to navigate unfamiliar territory, develop new patterns of life, and adjust to the responsibilities that come with freedom. They leave behind oppression, but they also leave behind predictability. The old structure is gone, and the new one has not yet fully taken shape.

That tension is often present in real life as well. Change can bring a mixture of relief and discomfort. A person may know that moving forward is necessary yet still grieve what has been lost or feel uncertain about what comes next. Growth often requires leaving behind what is familiar, and that process can feel disorienting even when it is good.

Reflecting on this question helps readers recognize that growth and discomfort often appear together. Understanding this connection can provide reassurance that moments of difficulty during times of change are not unusual but are often part of the process of moving toward a new stage of life. It can also help readers respond to transitions with more patience, honesty, and self-awareness.

Sometimes the hardest part of change is not the new challenge itself but the loss of identity that comes with leaving an old season behind. A person may no longer be who they were, yet not fully know who they are becoming. That space can feel vulnerable. It may involve grief, even when the transition is necessary and good. Exodus reflects that reality powerfully. The Israelites are no longer slaves, but they are not yet settled as a covenant people. They are in between.

That is why this question deserves honest reflection. Readers may ask themselves what part of change feels most difficult for them. Is it the loss of control? The uncertainty of outcomes? The discomfort of a new responsibility? The grief of leaving behind what once felt secure? Naming these challenges can reduce confusion and help a person move through transition with greater clarity.

How Do Moments of Uncertainty Shape Personal Growth?

Periods of uncertainty often become important moments of development, even though they may feel uncomfortable at the time. When individuals face situations where the outcome is unclear or the path forward is uncertain, they are often required to adapt in ways they may not have anticipated. These seasons can feel frustrating because they expose limitations, remove false confidence, and force people to confront questions they may have previously avoided.

At the same time, such moments can become powerful settings for growth. Uncertainty often pushes people to reflect more deeply, think more carefully, and respond with greater intentionality. It can reveal what they rely on, what they fear, and what matters most to them. Without clear answers, individuals may need to slow down, pay attention, and learn how to move forward with humility. Over time, these challenges can strengthen character and deepen a person's understanding of themselves and their priorities.

In Exodus, the wilderness becomes a place where the Israelites experience this kind of growth. The uncertainty of their environment forces them to learn new patterns of trust and dependence. What begins as a difficult period of transition eventually becomes a stage where the people begin to develop a stronger sense of identity and purpose. They are no longer simply reacting to Pharaoh's authority. They are gradually learning what it means to live as a people shaped by God's presence and instruction.

The same pattern often appears in modern life. A season that initially feels like confusion may later be recognized as a season of preparation. A difficult period may reveal strengths that would not have surfaced otherwise. Uncertainty can strip away illusions of control and create room for greater wisdom, patience, and resilience.

Reflecting on how uncertainty shapes personal growth allows readers to consider how difficult or confusing seasons in their own lives may also have contributed to the development of new strengths, insights, or perspectives. It invites them to ask not only what made a season hard, but also what that season may have formed within them.

This reflection can go even further. Readers may ask themselves whether uncertainty has exposed habits they need to confront, values they need to strengthen, or priorities they need to reorder. Unclear seasons often reveal whether a person's life has been built around comfort, appearance, control, or deeper convictions. In that sense, uncertainty is not only an obstacle. It can be a revealer.

Exodus helps readers see that growth is not always dramatic. Sometimes it occurs through repeated acts of endurance, small decisions to trust, and the slow reshaping of perspective. A person may not notice the change while it is happening, but over time, they may look back and realize they became steadier, wiser, less reactive, or more grounded than before. The wilderness did not simply test Israel. It also formed Israel.

What Role Does Trust Play When Facing Difficult Transitions?

Trust becomes especially important during times when circumstances are unclear and the future feels uncertain. When people face unfamiliar situations or major life transitions, they often rely on trust to continue moving forward. Without trust, uncertainty can become paralyzing. With trust, however, a person can keep taking steps even when the full picture is not yet visible.

This trust may take different forms. Some individuals place their trust in God and believe that guidance will emerge even when the path ahead is not fully visible. Others rely on supportive relationships, mentors, family members, or communities that provide encouragement and perspective during challenging times. Trust can also involve confidence that growth is taking place, even when immediate results are hard to see.

Trust is significant because transitions usually involve incomplete information. Rarely does a person know exactly how things will unfold. Instead, they must act with limited clarity, believing that the next step matters even if the final destination remains uncertain. That kind of movement requires more than optimism. It requires confidence placed somewhere—whether in God, in wise counsel, in deeply held convictions, or in the belief that the present difficulty will not have the final word.

The story of Exodus highlights the importance of trust as the Israelites travel through the wilderness. Their journey requires them to rely on guidance and provision that they cannot fully predict. Through these experiences, they gradually learn that trust often develops over time through repeated encounters with uncertainty and provision. They do not learn trust all at once. They learn it in stages, through moments of need, fear, rescue, and instruction.

Reflecting on the role of trust encourages readers to consider how faith, confidence, and support systems influence the way they respond to transitions and challenges in their own lives. It also invites them to ask where their trust is currently placed and whether that trust is helping them move forward with courage and steadiness.

This question can also reveal where trust is weak or divided. People sometimes say they trust, while quietly placing most of their confidence in control, prediction, approval, or visible results. Difficult transitions have a way of exposing that. They strip away easy certainty and reveal whether trust is truly rooted in something solid.

For readers, this makes trust a practical issue, not just a spiritual concept. Trust shapes how a person responds to delay, how they endure discomfort, how they make decisions under pressure, and how they treat others when life feels unstable. Exodus shows that trust is not built in comfort alone. It is built through repeated movement forward when certainty is limited. That makes trust not only comforting, but also strengthening.

What Lessons from Exodus Resonate Most Strongly with You?

The story of Exodus contains many themes that speak to readers in different ways. Some are drawn to the theme of liberation from slavery and the hope that change is possible even in difficult circumstances. Others connect more strongly with the challenges of transition and the uncertainty experienced during the wilderness journey. Still others find meaning in the themes of covenant, responsibility, leadership, worship, or God's presence among His people.

For some individuals, the most meaningful aspect of the story may be the idea of guidance and trust during periods of uncertainty. They may recognize in Exodus a reminder that growth often unfolds in stages and that God's presence does not disappear during difficult seasons. Others may focus on the importance of responsibility and purpose once freedom has been achieved, recognizing that real transformation involves more than escape. It requires learning how to live differently.

Because the narrative contains multiple layers of meaning, readers often find that different lessons stand out depending on their own experiences and the season of life they are currently navigating. A person facing hardship may be drawn to the theme of deliverance. A person in transition may resonate with the wilderness. A person carrying responsibility may notice the demands of leadership and covenant. In this way, Exodus continues to speak with fresh relevance because the story contains truths that meet readers in different places.

Taking time to identify the themes that resonate most strongly can help readers connect the ancient narrative with their personal experiences. Reflection becomes more meaningful when it is specific. Rather than simply admiring the story from a distance, readers begin to ask why certain parts stay with them and what those responses may reveal about their own lives.

Reflecting on these lessons encourages thoughtful engagement with the story and invites readers to consider how its message might influence their perspectives, decisions, and values moving forward. In this way, the reflection questions become an opportunity not only to think about the events described in Exodus but also to explore how its themes continue to shape understanding, purpose, and growth in modern life.

This question also encourages readers to pay attention to what they may be avoiding. Sometimes the lesson that resonates most strongly is the one that touches a current struggle. A person may find themselves drawn to leadership because they are facing responsibility, or to trust because they are living with uncertainty, or to freedom because they are waking up to patterns that have held them captive. Those responses can be revealing. They may point toward the area where the story is speaking most directly.

In the end, the goal of these questions is not merely analysis. It is reflection that leads to clearer living. Exodus is not simply meant to be understood at a distance. It is meant to be considered, remembered, and allowed to shape how readers interpret their own journeys. The more specifically they engage the story, the more clearly they may begin to see where it intersects with their present lives.

Chapter 10

Five Lessons

*"The Lord, the Lord, the compassionate and gracious God, slow
to anger, abounding in love and faithfulness."*
—Exodus 34:6

Exodus tells the story of a people moving from slavery to freedom, from chaos to covenant, and from survival to purpose. The narrative unfolds through dramatic moments—burning bushes, plagues, parted waters, wilderness journeys, and the formation of a nation learning how to live beyond oppression. Yet beneath the dramatic events lies something deeper than spectacle. Exodus is not only a story about escape. It is a story about transformation.

That's important because freedom alone does not automatically create a new life. People can leave the place that harmed them while still carrying the habits, fears, and patterns that formed there. Exodus shows that liberation may happen in a moment, but learning how to live freely takes time. The journey from Egypt to the promised future is not only geographical. It is personal, communal, and spiritual.

The characters in Exodus are not presented as perfect examples of courage or unwavering faith. They are people navigating uncertainty, fear, hope, and frustration. Moses wrestles with doubt about his ability to lead. The Israelites celebrate deliverance and then struggle when the path becomes difficult. Their story reflects the complexity of human response to change. Freedom can inspire gratitude, but it can also reveal anxieties that were hidden while survival was the only concern.

These experiences reveal patterns that remain familiar today.

Modern life often celebrates the idea of breakthrough moments when obstacles disappear, and progress suddenly becomes possible. But real transformation rarely unfolds that cleanly. People still struggle to leave unhealthy environments, to build new habits after difficult seasons, and to trust a path that feels uncertain. Exodus reminds readers that change involves movement, patience, and resilience.

The journey through the wilderness becomes a place where character is shaped. Courage begins the journey, but endurance sustains it. Faith grows through uncertainty. Leadership develops through responsibility. And freedom itself becomes something that must be learned.

Several insights emerge repeatedly throughout the narrative. These are not abstract ideas. They grow out of conflict, struggle, and hard-earned experience. Exodus teaches through movement—through confrontation with power, through moments of fear and faith, through the long road between rescue and renewal.

1. Freedom Often Begins with Courage

Freedom rarely begins with comfort. More often, it begins with a moment when someone chooses to move forward despite fear. People frequently remain in harmful or restrictive circumstances because the uncertainty of change feels overwhelming. Even when a situation is clearly unhealthy, the familiar can feel safer than the unknown.

Human beings naturally seek stability. When facing major decisions, people imagine what might go wrong—loss of security, strained relationships, or the possibility of failure. These fears can create powerful resistance, even when remaining in the current situation is no longer sustainable.

Courage does not mean the absence of fear. It means deciding that the possibility of a better future is worth the risk of stepping forward.

The story of Exodus reflects this reality. Moses confronts Pharaoh despite his doubts and the immense power Pharaoh represents. The Israelites also face a difficult decision. Leaving Egypt means stepping away from the only environment they have known. Even though their lives there were marked by injustice, Egypt still represents familiarity. The wilderness represents uncertainty.

Yet movement begins when they act.

Exodus reminds readers that courage is often quieter than people expect. It may appear as telling the truth after a long silence, ending a destructive pattern, asking for help, or taking responsibility for a difficult task. These choices may feel small, but they open the path toward transformation.

Freedom often begins with a simple decision: fear will no longer determine the direction of life.

2. Change Rarely Happens Instantly

Moments of breakthrough can create the expectation that transformation will happen immediately. When people experience a turning point, they often assume the difficulties that once surrounded them will quickly disappear.

Exodus presents a different reality.

The Israelites experience a dramatic moment of liberation when they leave Egypt, but that moment does not complete their transformation. Instead, it begins a long process of learning how to live as a free people. The wilderness becomes a place of adjustment, growth, and formation.

During this journey, the Israelites must develop new habits, learn new patterns of life, and understand what it means to live without oppression shaping their identity. At times, they express hope and excitement. At other times, they struggle with doubt and nostalgia for the past.

These mixed responses reflect a common human experience. Leaving an old life does not automatically create a new one.

Real change usually unfolds gradually. It requires patience, repeated effort, and the willingness to continue moving forward even when progress feels slow.

Exodus teaches that transformation is rarely defined by a single dramatic moment. More often, it is shaped by a long series of faithful steps.

3. Faith Develops Through Challenges

Faith often grows most deeply during moments of uncertainty. When life unfolds according to expectations, trust may remain largely untested. But when circumstances become difficult or unpredictable, people are forced to consider what they truly rely on.

The wilderness journey in Exodus repeatedly places the Israelites in situations where fear and trust compete for control. They worry about survival, question their direction, and struggle to maintain confidence in the path ahead.

These reactions reveal a deeper truth: faith is not simply a belief held in comfortable circumstances. It develops through lived experience.

Trust grows when people encounter difficulty and discover that guidance, provision, or strength emerges along the way. Challenges do not automatically produce faith, but they create the conditions where faith can deepen.

Exodus also emphasizes the importance of remembering. The Israelites are repeatedly reminded to recall what God has already done. Memory becomes a source of strength when the future feels uncertain.

In this way, faith develops through both struggle and remembrance. Hardship exposes human limits, but it can also create opportunities to experience help that might otherwise remain unseen.

4. Leadership Requires Humility and Persistence

Moses does not begin his leadership with confidence. When he is called to lead the Israelites, his first response is hesitation. He questions his abilities, worries about how others will respond, and doubts his own readiness.

This humility becomes an important part of his leadership.

Throughout the journey, Moses faces criticism, conflict, and moments of uncertainty. Leading the Israelites requires patience, resilience, and the willingness to guide people through circumstances that are often confusing and frustrating.

Exodus portrays leadership not as effortless authority but as steady perseverance. Moses continues forward even when progress is slow and opposition arises.

This perspective challenges common assumptions about leadership. Modern culture often associates leadership with charisma, confidence, or visibility. Exodus highlights something different: humility, endurance, and dependence on guidance beyond oneself.

Leadership also involves growth. Moses develops through the journey. His story reminds readers that leaders are not fully formed at the beginning of their responsibilities. They mature through experience, persistence, and a willingness to keep learning.

5. True Freedom Includes Responsibility

Freedom is often described as the removal of restrictions or the ability to make independent choices. Exodus shows that freedom involves something more. Liberation creates opportunity, but it also brings responsibility.

After leaving Egypt, the Israelites are not simply released into a life without structure. They are given laws and teachings that shape how they live as a community. These instructions guide their relationships, encourage justice, and define how freedom should be expressed.

This structure helps prevent freedom from becoming disorder. When individuals act without considering how their choices affect others, communities can become unstable. Shared principles provide the framework needed for freedom to flourish.

Exodus presents freedom as relational rather than purely individual. The way one person uses freedom influences the well-being of others.

Responsibility does not limit freedom; it protects and sustains it.

The journey of the Israelites illustrates that freedom reaches its fullest meaning when it is guided by wisdom, purpose, and care for others. Courage begins the journey. Patience sustains it. Faith deepens through challenge. Leadership helps guide it. Responsibility gives it direction.

Together, these lessons reveal a larger truth: freedom is not only a gift to receive. It is a life to learn and live.

The Lessons Hold

Exodus ends with a people no longer defined by slavery but still learning what freedom means. The journey from Egypt has begun, but the full promise of their future is still unfolding. The wilderness has shaped them, challenged them, and begun forming them into a community with purpose.

That is why the story continues to matter.

Freedom often begins with courage.

Change rarely happens instantly.

Faith develops through challenges.

Leadership requires humility and persistence.

And true freedom includes responsibility.

These lessons are not confined to ancient deserts or distant history. They remain present wherever people confront fear, seek change, wrestle with uncertainty, and try to build lives defined by purpose rather than survival.

Exodus reminds us that the journey toward freedom is rarely simple. It involves risk, patience, and growth. Yet it also reveals something enduring about the human story: people are capable of transformation. When courage begins the journey, and responsibility guides the path, freedom becomes more than escape. It becomes the foundation for a new way of living.

Closing Reflection

"Then the cloud covered the tent of meeting, and the glory of the Lord filled the tabernacle. Moses could not enter the tent of meeting because the cloud had settled on it, and the glory of the Lord filled the tabernacle.

In all the travels of the Israelites, whenever the cloud lifted from above the tabernacle, they would set out; but if the cloud did not lift, they did not set out—until the day it lifted. So the cloud of the Lord was over the tabernacle by day, and fire was in the cloud by night, in the sight of all the Israelites during all their travels."
— Exodus 40:34–38

Exodus tells the story of a people learning what it means to move from slavery to freedom. At the beginning of the narrative, the Israelites live under harsh conditions in Egypt, bound to a system that controls their labor and limits their future. Their lives are shaped by forces beyond their control, and their daily existence is defined by the demands of an empire that views them primarily as a source of labor rather than as a community with dignity, purpose, and identity.

Generations of Israelites grow up knowing nothing but this environment. The structures of Egyptian authority shape how they live, how they work, and how they understand their place in the world. Their story begins in a setting where hope appears limited, and the possibility of change seems distant. The weight of bondage affects not only their physical lives but also the way they imagine the future.

Over time, however, a series of dramatic events unfolds that leads them out of that environment and into a new stage of their history. Through the leadership of Moses and the intervention of God, the Israelites are delivered from the authority of Pharaoh and begin a journey that will reshape their identity as a people. The dramatic events surrounding their departure from Egypt mark one of the most powerful turning points in the biblical narrative.

The story traces their movement from slavery toward liberation. Yet it also shows that freedom is not simply a single moment of escape. Instead, it marks the beginning of a much larger process in which the people must discover how to live differently and how to shape a new identity for themselves. Leaving Egypt changes their circumstances, but it does not immediately define who they will become.

In this sense, Exodus is not only a story about rescue. It is a story about transformation. The Israelites must move beyond the conditions that once defined them and begin learning how to live with the freedom that has been placed before them.

This opening movement of the story remains relevant because it captures a truth many people know from experience: sometimes the first major change in life is external, but the deeper work still lies ahead. A person can be removed from one kind of bondage and still need time, guidance, and growth to become fully free. Exodus understands that freedom is not merely a change of location. It is a change of identity, direction, and way of life.

The Journey Beyond Liberation

As the narrative develops, the Israelites learn that leaving slavery behind does not automatically answer every question about the future. Their departure from Egypt marks the start of a journey filled with uncertainty, unfamiliar landscapes, and difficult decisions. The road ahead does not lead immediately to comfort or stability. Instead, it leads into the wilderness.

The wilderness journey becomes an environment where the people must adjust to new realities. The structure that once defined their lives in Egypt has disappeared, and they must now learn how to organize themselves in a completely different way. No longer controlled by taskmasters, they must begin discovering how to live as a community responsible for its own direction and choices.

During this time, they begin to develop a clearer understanding of their relationship with God and the responsibilities that accompany their freedom. The guidance they receive at Mount Sinai introduces new principles that shape how they live, how they relate to one another, and how they understand their purpose.

Through moments of challenge, instruction, and reflection, the Israelites gradually form the foundations of a society built not on subjugation but on covenant, guidance, and shared responsibility. Their identity begins to take shape through the lessons they learn along the way. The wilderness becomes a place not only of difficulty but also of formation.

This stage of the story reveals that liberation is only the first step. The work of transformation occurs as the people begin to build a new way of life beyond the systems that once defined them.

The same pattern appears again and again in human life. People often long for deliverance from something painful, restrictive, or unjust, and that longing is real. Yet once the moment of change arrives, new questions quickly follow. How should life now be lived? What should replace the old habits, fears, and structures? What kind of future should be built from the freedom that has been gained? Exodus does not avoid those questions. It moves directly into them.

Freedom and Responsibility

In this way, Exodus reminds readers that liberation is only the beginning of a larger journey. The dramatic events that free the Israelites from Egypt create an opportunity for change, but the transformation of the people unfolds gradually as they move forward.

Their experiences demonstrate that freedom brings both possibility and responsibility. Deliverance opens the door to new opportunities, but it also requires individuals and communities to make thoughtful choices about how they will live. Freedom removes external control, yet it introduces new responsibilities related to self-governance, moral decisions, and shared values.

The story emphasizes that what people choose to do with their freedom ultimately shapes the direction of their lives and the character of their community. Freedom provides the opportunity to build something new, but that process requires wisdom, discipline, and a commitment to shared principles.

Without responsibility, freedom can easily become chaotic or destructive. The instructions given at Mount Sinai illustrate how structure and guidance help preserve the benefits of liberation. The people are invited to create a society grounded in justice, respect, and devotion to God.

In this way, Exodus teaches that freedom reaches its fullest meaning when it is guided by purpose and responsibility.

This lesson remains especially important because modern people often speak about freedom as if it were valuable for its own sake alone. Exodus offers a more complete vision. Freedom matters, but what matters just as much is what people do with it. The question is not only whether chains have been removed. The question is whether life is being built on something strong, true, and good after those chains are gone.

Building a Life After Freedom

The book challenges readers to think carefully about the kind of lives they build once freedom becomes possible. Moments of deliverance or opportunity create space for new choices, but those choices require reflection and intention.

Exodus encourages readers to consider how they respond when circumstances change and when new responsibilities appear. It invites thoughtful reflection on the values that guide individual decisions and the ways communities develop systems that promote justice, trust, and cooperation.

Freedom alone does not guarantee a meaningful future. Individuals and communities must actively shape the direction they wish to pursue. The habits, relationships, and commitments developed after liberation become the foundation upon which future generations will build.

The narrative raises questions about how people create meaningful lives after periods of struggle. It highlights the importance of developing relationships, habits, and structures that support stability and growth. In doing so, it invites readers to reflect on how they themselves respond when new opportunities arise.

It also reminds readers that a meaningful life is rarely built by accident. It is formed through repeated choices, daily commitments, and a willingness to align actions with values. The Israelites had to become the kind of people who could live in the freedom they had been given. Readers today face the same challenge in their own way. Opportunity creates potential, but character and direction determine what becomes of that potential.

The Wilderness as a Place of Growth

These questions remain meaningful because the journey described in Exodus mirrors many experiences people face in their own lives. Periods of transition often involve uncertainty, growth, and the need to adapt to unfamiliar situations.

Just as the Israelites had to learn how to navigate the wilderness and rely on guidance along the way, individuals today frequently encounter moments when they must move forward without fully knowing what the future holds. These seasons can feel uncomfortable because the stability of the past has disappeared while the shape of the future remains unclear.

During such times people may experience doubt, hesitation, or fear as they attempt to make sense of their circumstances. They may question their direction or struggle to maintain confidence when progress appears slow.

The story of Exodus invites readers to reflect on how they approach such moments and what attitudes or values guide their decisions during times of change. It suggests that seasons of uncertainty can become opportunities for learning, reflection, and personal development.

The wilderness, rather than being a place of failure, becomes a place of formation.

That may be one of the most encouraging parts of the book. The wilderness is not where the story falls apart. It is where the real work happens. It is where trust is tested, identity is clarified, and dependence on God becomes more real. For readers living in their own kind of wilderness, that truth carries weight. It means an unclear season is not necessarily an empty one.

Transformation in Unexpected Places

For modern readers, Exodus continues to serve as a powerful reminder that transformation often begins in unexpected ways. The Israelites' journey does not start with a clear plan or a predictable path. Instead, it begins with a series of events that challenge the power structures of Egypt and open the door to a new future.

The process of change unfolds gradually, often through situations that test the patience and faith of those involved. What initially appears as a series of difficulties eventually becomes the pathway toward a new identity and purpose.

This pattern reflects a broader truth about life. Meaningful transformation frequently emerges from circumstances that initially appear uncertain or challenging. Moments of disruption can sometimes create opportunities for growth that would not have been possible otherwise.

What begins as hardship may eventually become the starting point for renewal and discovery.

That does not mean hardship is easy or desirable. Exodus never treats suffering lightly. But it does show that painful beginnings do not have to determine the final outcome. A season that feels marked by limitation can still become the place where something new is born. A moment of collapse can become the first step toward rebuilding on stronger ground.

Growth Through Struggle

At the same time, the narrative acknowledges that the journey toward purpose is rarely simple. The Israelites encounter obstacles, frustrations, and moments of doubt along the way. Their path includes times when they question the direction they are taking and struggle to trust the guidance they receive.

These experiences reveal that growth often involves setbacks and learning experiences that shape a person's character over time. The journey toward maturity and understanding is rarely a straight line. Instead, it often includes moments of progress as well as moments of uncertainty.

By portraying these struggles honestly, the story avoids presenting transformation as effortless or immediate. Instead, it acknowledges the complexity of human growth and the patience required to navigate life's challenges.

This realism is one reason the story continues to resonate with readers. It reflects the reality that growth often emerges through perseverance rather than perfection.

In that way, Exodus offers both challenge and comfort. It challenges readers not to expect easy transformation. But it also comforts them by showing that struggle does not mean the process has failed. Often struggle is part of the process itself. The people of Exodus do not become who they are meant to be despite the difficulty. In many ways, they are formed through it.

A Message of Hope

Yet within these challenges, the book also carries a message of hope. Even in the most difficult circumstances, the story suggests that new paths can emerge and a future can take shape.

The Israelites' experience demonstrates that situations that seem fixed or hopeless can change in ways that open unexpected possibilities. Their journey from slavery toward freedom becomes a reminder that hardship does not necessarily determine the final outcome of a story.

For readers reflecting on their own lives, this message can provide encouragement during seasons of difficulty or uncertainty. The narrative of Exodus invites people to see their struggles not only as obstacles but also as moments that may lead to growth, renewal, and the discovery of new direction.

By tracing the journey of a people who move from slavery toward purpose, the book offers a vision of hope grounded in the belief that transformation is possible and that the future can hold possibilities beyond what seems visible in the present.

In this way, Exodus continues to speak across generations. It reminds readers that the path toward freedom, identity, and purpose may involve uncertainty and struggle, but it also holds the possibility of renewal, growth, and a future shaped by hope.

And perhaps that is where the book leaves its deepest impression. Exodus does not promise a life without wilderness, difficulty, or unanswered questions. What it does offer is something stronger: the assurance that bondage is not the end of the story, that uncertainty can become formation, and that God's presence can guide people through seasons they do not fully understand. That is why Exodus remains more than an ancient text. It remains a living reminder that even when the road is hard and the outcome is not yet visible, the journey toward freedom and purpose is still possible.

The Bible for Modern Life Series

This book is part of **The Bible for Modern Life** series—an ongoing collection that explores the meaning, historical setting, and message of individual books of Scripture.

Each volume looks closely at the biblical text to help readers understand what it meant in its original context and how its truths still apply to life today.

The goal is simple: to help modern readers engage more deeply with the Bible—one book at a time.

— Samuel Whitaker